TRUE CONFESSIONS WEDNESDAY

THOUGHTS FROM AN ORGANIZATIONAL WORK
IN PROGRESS

LISA LAWMASTER HESS

INTRODUCTION

Welcome to my organizing confessions!

As I closed in on five years of posts at Organizing by STYLE, I was looking for something new. I wanted something that focused on organization, but that also let readers know more about the person behind the posts. All along, I've told readers that I'm someone in the trenches with them — an organizational work-in-progress — and I wanted this new set of posts to share some of the ways that is true, along with the real life examples regular readers have come to expect.

So, I introduced a recurring Wednesday feature called True Confessions Wednesday. I had so much fun with it that, before I knew it, I hit the 50 post mark. That seemed like a good time to gather the posts together into a book.

What follows is a lightly edited version of the posts you can find mixed in with a variety of other posts on my Organizing by STYLE blog (www.orgbystyle.blogspot.com). A mix of confession and advice, each post lets you know something about me and how I employ the organizing by STYLE methods I describe in my book, *Know Thyself: The Imper-*

fectionist's Guide to Sorting Your Stuff — and where I struggle because, after all, it's a process.

Before we dig in, let me share some background information that will make these entries clearer for those who aren't regular readers. When I write about Organizing by STYLE, there are three styles at work: personal styles, organizational styles, and the STYLE process. For the sake of brevity, I've outlined them below.

Personal styles (the personality element): *I need to see it, I love stuff, I love to be busy*

Organizational styles (the nuts and bolts): *drop & run, cram & jam, I know I put it somewhere*

STYLE (the process):

Start with successes

Take small steps

Yes, it has a home

Let it go!

Easy upkeep

Want a little more information on the personal and organizational styles? Check out the Personal and Organizational Styles quiz on my Organizing by STYLE blog.

Want more than that? Visit my blog, Organizing by STYLE. If you click on the *Know Thyself* tab at the top of the home page, you'll be able to read a sample that describes the personal and organizational styles.

Happy reading — and organizing — by STYLE, of course! Just remember: it's a process.

True Confession #1: I'm a container collector.

ONE WEEKEND, as I was working on decluttering my office, I realized that the magazine holders I was using to corral my notebooks were the wrong tool for the job. Fortunately, I only had to go my basement to find an appropriate replacement.

Okay, I admit it. I love to wander the container aisles of, well, pretty much any store. Unless I'm in search of a particular item, though, I go home empty-handed most of the time, a result that has more to do with my container collection than a high degree of self-control. Between the bags and organizers I have left over from my days selling Thirty-One gifts and the office/paper organizers I have left over from my days as a school counselor teaching organizational skills to elementary school students, I have quite the selection on hand in my basement. When I don't have the tool that's "just right," I go shopping (excitedly and without hesitation) but, most of the time, I check the inventory in my basement before I buy. I have a particular weakness for paper storage products, along with unique containers and, of course, bargains. Consequently, when I give in to temptation and buy something to add to my collection, it's usually out of dollar bins (or at the dollar store) or in the office supply aisle.

Last weekend, I was grateful for my collection. Within fifteen minutes of identifying the container as the problem, I'd found something better, replaced the magazine holders and improved the look of the counter in my office.

Did I get rid of the magazine holders? Please. They were perfectly reusable. Just because they didn't work in the office doesn't mean they won't work somewhere else.

So, into the basement they went because, after all, there's nothing quite like a container that's a perfect fit.

True Confession #2: I'm a big fan of the small steps approach.

LIKE MANY PEOPLE, when I find something overwhelming, I put off doing it. When I finally get to the task, it's usually a lot easier than I made it. Sometimes, the key to getting to the task faster is to baby step my way in.

A little over a week ago, when I decided to approach the junk drawer in my dining room slowly, I set a goal for removing and finding homes for five items each day. It seemed reasonable.

Actually, if I'm to be honest, it sounded a little pathetic.

Five items? At that rate, it would take weeks.

Cocky, I dug into the drawer, sure that getting started was the hard part and I'd exceed my five-item goal without breaking a sweat.

I promptly discovered that a goal of five items was just about right.

As it turns out, what was in the drawer wasn't entirely junk; it was a collection of homeless items ranging from the sentimental to the financial. In other words, a lot of it was stuff I have to keep. And find new, logical homes for.

Cleaning out a junk drawer sounds easy enough. If the items in the drawer are really just junk, they're easily disposed of. What I had on my hands, however, was a catchall drawer, which is little more than a collection of *I need to see it* piles stashed out of sight.

Ugh. What was I thinking?

As the week went on, the job got easier and on many days I did, indeed, clear out far more than five items. By the middle of last week, the job was done and I'd moved on to other challenging spots, taking my five things rule with me.

If time doesn't permit us to tackle a big spot all at once,

or a decluttering job is too daunting, taking small steps can be just what we need. Five things is better than no things and slowly, but surely, we can begin to see progress, which is often just what we need to dig in more deeply.

Five things each day, one thing each time we pass by or any other small step can also lead us to the develop the habit of picking up as we go. On several occasions, I've heard comedian Jerry Seinfeld's "don't break the chain" advice. As the story goes, Seinfeld advised young comics to put a big, red X on the calendar for each day that they wrote. As they got into the habit of writing daily, the calendar would begin to fill with those Xs. Their goal then became not breaking the chain and, the way to do that was to write every day.

Similarly, a chain of days where we pick up and find homes for five things in a pile can lead us to find homes for a lot of things (and clear a lot of space) if we stick to it.

So, as it turns out, that perfectionistic little voice in my brain that scolds me about starting too small needs a mute button.

And I have the empty drawer to prove it.

True Confession #3: I love to organize.

I DON'T MIND cleaning and I tolerate cooking, but I truly love to organize. I find clear spaces refreshing. I love sorting (and tossing) and finding the just right container.

It's a good thing, too. As a writer and educator, I work in two paper-intensive professions, which means there is rarely a shortage of paper clutter in my house. As someone with an *I need to see it* personal style, I remain a paper-and-pencil girl, too, and am unlikely to reduce the deluge of paper by going electronic.

Since I've begun organizing by STYLE, I've gotten much better about choosing the tools and containers that work for me. Binders and file cabinets are wonderful tools — for someone else. For me, they're just clutter catchers. I do much better when I choose smaller containers that force me to not only be selective about what goes in, but also to purge on a regular basis, lest I run out of room (because I never seem to run out of papers). I prefer containers that are open (that's my *drop and run* organizational style speaking), but also do well with clear drawers and drawers that can be labeled.

But the biggest contributor to staying organized is developing the habits to go with the tools. Getting in the habit of putting something away instead of down. Getting in the habit of consistently putting the same item in the same place. Breaking the habit of using tools that don't work for me, no matter how pretty, decorative or well-suited to someone else they may be.

I grew up in a house where everything looked neat all the time, a house that bears little resemblance to my own very lived-in little house. When I was a young adult, I reveled in the pendulum swing of my own declaration of independence, evidenced by my joy over being able to leave anything wherever I wanted to. Now, although I'm completely able to appreciate the beauty of a clear, well-organized space, I also want the ease that comes with achieving that in a way that works for me, even if that includes leaving something on the dining room table so I don't forget it has to be done. I want to feel comfortable in my own living space, even if it's imperfect (which it always is). Even if I'm imperfect.

Before I accepted my styles (instead of trying to fit myself into other people's), organizing was an obligation -- something externally imposed and somewhat burdensome. Now, having discovered what truly works for me on a regular basis, organizing is something I look forward to. No longer a chore, it's now a challenge -- and one I've proven I can rise to.

What's not to love?

True Confession #4: I am a global thinker.

I LOVE THE IDEA STAGE, the blank page, the place where everything is possible.

It's the details I hate. Whoever said the devil is in the details had it right. It's the details I stress over. Afraid I won't get it right, or I'll miss something or head completely in the wrong direction, I waste my time on worry and end up draining the energy I could have spent *on* the details *avoiding* them.

It's a vicious circle.

One of the things I love about style-based organizing is that I don't have to immediately get the details right. I can observe and experiment, playing with possible solutions until I find the Goldilocks solution — the one that's "just right."

This frustration with the details is exacerbated by my lack of patience. When I have plenty of time or the stakes are low, I don't really mind working out the details. But, since the big picture is my strong suit, I rarely find myself in that position; avoiding the details comes much more naturally. Determining the details takes so much time and energy that I want to just throw my hands up and abdicate responsibility of the detail-determining to someone who's good at it.

Like my husband.

You might think it's good that a global thinker is married to a detail-oriented person and, sometimes, you'd be right. Other times?

Well, you know how it works with oil and water. The same can be said for organizing opposites, which makes things interesting in shared spaces.

It's a process.

True Confession #5: I'm a pack-as-you-go kinda girl.

IN THE FIRST year seminar I teach, we watch Adam Grant's TED Talk about "originals" which includes the concept of pre-crastination — that laudable habit of starting in on something right away, as soon as possible.

Yeah. I don't have that. At least not most of the time.

But, when it comes to packing for a trip, my husband comes pretty close. Sure, he doesn't start packing the minute after the reservation is confirmed, but he usually begins his preparations at least a week in advance.

I do not do this. I'm a procrastinator under many circumstances, but packing probably tops the list. As someone with an *I need to see it* personal style, my packing plan can be loosely described as, "it gets worse before it gets better."

I suspect that my approach makes him uncomfortable, and I know his approach pricks at my conscience. If I'm not careful, it can also get the shoulds rolling.

But I've learned over time that my method works — or qualifies as workable, at least — for me.

The first step in my packing process is the mental list — thinking through what I want to bring along. Sometimes I do this at night before I fall asleep, which kinda rules out making actual lists. Other times, I do it during normal waking hours and actually write things down.

As I write this, we're preparing for a trip. Earlier today, I seriously considered packing only clean underwear and toiletries in my suitcase and bringing my dirty clothes in a laundry bag. Then, I can wash them when we arrive and, voilà! Outfits.

In some ways, this plan seems so much easier — I mean, my clothes in the laundry bag aren't mud-encrusted or gross or anything — and I'd avoid generating additional dirty laundry. Though I'm leaning toward something more traditional, I'd be lying if I said I'd ruled out the laundry bag plan entirely.

The second step in my somewhat organized personal packing plan (the one that involves only clean clothes) is making sure everything I want to pack/wear while I'm away is already clean and packable. This step is an integral part of the whole process of planning what to pack.

Sometime over the next few days, I'll get serious. Clean, seasonally appropriate clothing that can be mixed and matched will make it into a bag. I will wait, though, because the longer it's in the suitcase, the more wrinkled it becomes, and my make-up and some of my toiletries (the ones I haven't pre-packed) will be the last things to go in the bag.

Do I forget things? If I'm honest, the answer is yes, I sometimes do, *but* I usually don't forget the really important stuff. That's the stuff that makes it onto a list or gets packed first.

There are lots of reasons for my approach to packing, but that's another post. As for this trip and this approach, I'm currently at the plan-and-pile stage.

Seems only appropriate for an *I need to see it* girl.

True Confession #6: I love hotel rooms and vacation spaces.

ASIDE FROM THE fact that being in one of these places usually means I'm taking a break for fun and/or learning, I love how easy it is to be organized in these spaces.

First of all, the sheer amount of stuff I have with me is minimized, limited to only what I could fit in the suitcase and various tote bags I packed specifically for the occasion. Hanging my clothes up is something I *want* to do because the alternative is to leave them crumpled up in my suitcase.

Not cool.

Second, these spaces are compartmentalized. There's the closet (for clothes), the desk (for my laptop and other work materials), the bed (for sleeping), the bathroom (for toiletries and makeup), and, if I'm lucky, some sort of reading chair/sofa/side table combination (for leisure). Figuring out where everything goes is easy which means that most of the time, everything is either where I packed it (where I left it last) or where it belongs. *Everything.* Nothing is homeless and, as long as I packed it, it has to be in the room somewhere.

I also designate spots for things like chargers (the one for my laptop is with my laptop and the one for my phone is usually on the desk as well) and my room key. Putting things in the same spot each time saves search time and, in addition, helps to create the habit of taking what I need with me when I go.

Last weekend, we were at the beach. We stay at the same condo complex each time and the number of rooms and their composition/layout are pretty similar from one unit to the next. This allows me to do the same type of organizing in this much larger space as I do in a hotel room.

While it might seem silly to focus on organization while I'm on vacation, for me, this predictability and consistency (not to mention knowing where to find my things) contributes to a sense of relaxation. It's not really surprising that that is the case since the same thing is true at home. The better organized I am and the less stuff I have laying around, the less stressed I feel.

How about you? When you take a vacation, do you take a vacation from organization, too?

True Confession #7: When I get busy, I get stuck in a push-pull between things that are deadline-driven and things that aren't.

MY DINING ROOM table is currently in serious need of intervention. We went away the weekend before last and have another trip coming up. My dining room, which sits in the center of our house, has a lovely table that is supposed to be used for eating but is currently too full of my various piles of things to perform that function.

It started small, as I began preparing for our trip to the beach, which collided with mid-semester assignments and warning grades. Papers to grade, grading sheets and class prep information took up residence, then disappeared gradually as I finished grading and returned the papers to their rightful owners. I dropped a few odds and ends — extra grading sheets, blank copies of exams — and ran, assuming I'd return all of those items to their various homes shortly.

Then, we got home from the beach, picked up the mail and started unpacking (not necessarily in that order). Nonessential mail (magazines, catalogs) landed "temporarily" on the table, keeping the school odds and ends company. Then, I went shopping for prizes for an online party and laid all of those things out on the table because I need to see things. After the party, I packed them up and took them to the post office but, again, a few stray items remained.

Now, we're planning a trip to go see our daughter at college. As I come across things I want to take along, I put them in a pile — you guessed it — on the dining room table.

Every time I walk by that table, I cringe. I also aim to pick up something and put it away every time I pass but, no sooner do I clear off a space than a new *I need to see it* task arises and something else gets dropped into that freshly decluttered location.

Meanwhile, life moves forward. New tasks with deadlines arise and the old task of clearing off my table (which has no external deadline) gets pushed aside as the clutter expands.

And therein lies the problem.

I rarely miss a deadline of someone else's making. While this may be admirable, professional, or whatever else you may call it, it often happens at the expense of deadlines I've set for myself. And, when things get too busy, I stop setting personal deadlines altogether. Stuck in survival mode, I keep moving forward only to drag hot spots like my dining room table along behind me like so much baggage. Sprinkle in a few surprises like an unexpected crisis, illness, or phone call, and that baggage just gets heavier. Or, worse yet, it gets abandoned in favor of mindless television or something equally non-demanding.

Just me?

I wish I could say I had an easy answer to this, but there is no easy fix. I can try not to let things pile up in the first place and, to an extent, I do. I can make sure I finish one task before starting another, something that's a major challenge for those of us with a *drop and run* organizational style. I can try not to overbook myself, bringing myself one step closer to finishing what I start, but I can't control the unexpected interruptions. All I can do is decide whether or not to engage in them.

Once the clutter gets dropped onto the surface, there is nothing to do but chip away at it and do my best not to add to it. These are the times I employ **Give it Five!**, or pick up one thing every time I walk past, or tackle the table one pile at a time.

Life happens. And for me, the more that's going on, the more likely I am to end up with piles. As there is nothing in my life I want to get rid of (cooking dinner notwithstanding), all I can do is try to keep on top of the habits that create the clutter and, once it appears, tackle it one stack at at time.

True Confession #8: My *I need to see it* personal style is abundantly in evidence in my home -- especially when no one else is home.

IN THE DECADE in which I've been perfecting the art of matching my styles to matching my organizational systems, I've come up with a lot of tools that work for me. While these tools keep my piling somewhat under control, my default piles still pop up and serve a purpose — one that's useful to me, if not to the other people who live with me.

Three days a week, I finish teaching at noon, which (theoretically) means I have the afternoon at home to work on...whatever. On Monday, when I left for work, I left a bottle of nasal spray on the bathroom counter (to remind myself to call the pharmacy for a refill), a small pile of dirty clothes by the door to the basement (to remind myself to move the laundry from the washer to the dryer) and a variety of items on my dining room table that I half hoped would jump out at me to make sure I didn't ignore them.

It wasn't pretty.

As an empty nester in a two-income household, most days I'm the last to leave the house in the morning and the first to arrive home. This means I can pick up all my "reminders" before anyone else sees them, making it a workable (if less than visually appealing) system — for me at least.

Occasionally, my husband arrives home before I do and discovers my "system." I'm sure that to him these appear to be miscellaneous items left carelessly lying about. To his credit, he never says as much, but I still feel like a kid caught with her hand in the cookie jar on a very cluttered counter.

When I have to (other people are home, company is

coming), I use lists instead, but this shorthanded here-a-reminder, there-a-reminder approach nudges me more than any list does. And most of the time, I accomplish these tasks because doing the task the thing I left out reminds me to do always ends the same way: I put away the reminder item, leaving only clear space in its wake.

If our schedules ever change, I might reconsider this approach but, as long as I'm the last one out and the first one back, I don't see any harm in a few visual reminders, especially if they help me get the job done.

What less-than-ideal systems are you reluctant to let go of?

True confession #9: I don't always love my styles.

NO, I'm not renouncing everything I've been saying all along. I've learned to embrace my styles, to utilize them, and to create strategies that work with them. All of these things have contributed to me being much more organized with much less effort.

But, when I am overwhelmed and time is short, I revert to their less useful side. I start to drop and run. Instead of trusting my well-crafted lists, I allow reminders to collect in piles because there is a certain solace in seeing what needs to be done and an even greater satisfaction in putting it all away just so when the tasks are complete.

Still, it frustrates me that things aren't perfect, leading me to overlook a not-so-obvious fact.

Every style has both flaws and attributes.

On the plus side, my *I need to see it* personal style has led me to take color coding to a whole new level while recognizing my *drop and run* organizational style has removed my guilt over not using tools like binders and file cabinets well. More important, understanding my styles has brought me to a larger conclusion: that things like binders and file cabinets are simply tools. I they don't work for me, I'm not broken. I just need a different tool.

This is true for the other styles as well. Those with a *cram and jam* organizational style are great at utilizing space – especially small spaces — and consistently putting things in the same place. Learning to transfer those concepts to organizational systems that don't leave things squished and smashed and torn allows cram and jammers to put what comes naturally to work.

Those who put things in safe places (those with an *I*

know I put it somewhere organizational style) have the basic concept of putting things away and need only to become more methodical in that practice. People who embody the *I love to be busy* personal style often manage time very well; working toward managing their space with the same efficiency and utilizing small pockets of time to do so polishes that strength. Finally, those with an *I love stuff* personal style have the gift of seeing treasure in mundane things.

When piles abound or we can't remember what safe place we put something in or our things are wrinkled and torn from being stuffed into a too-small space, it's hard to embrace our styles with acceptance and gratitude. But, the more we work *with* our two-sided styles instead of trying to fight *against* them, the easier it becomes to be thankful for them, warts and all.

And the better organized we become.

True Confession #10: I am an organizational work-in-progress.

IF YOU ARE A REGULAR READER, you know this is something I blithely admit on a regular basis. Last weekend, however, someone else pointed it out to me and hearing it felt like a sucker punch.

The person who pointed it out to me was my daughter and the way she put it was, well, blunt. "Your stuff is everywhere, Mom."

My first instinct was to deny, but a quick look around the room where we sat made that impossible. Shame quickly followed, along with embarrassment and the sense that I'm a fraud. I mean, I write about this stuff. How could I have let this happen??

Life, that's how.

The past few weeks have been a succession of interruptions, quasi-emergencies and routine-busting crises. I've fallen behind in pretty much every conceivable area of life.

Now, approaching the other side of the tunnel I've been in, I can see the light, but it's shining on piles that reveal just how quickly even someone who knows her styles and knows how to use them can fall back into bad habits.

Every style has attributes and downfalls. While I was putting out proverbial fires, my downfalls were having a party and they didn't even have the decency to contain it to one room of the house.

When I set out to teach these styles to my students and, later, write *Know Thyself,* I had two goals. One of them was to help people who struggle with organization to find systems that work for them for more than two days. The other was to disabuse them of the notion that there was something wrong with them because they weren't flawlessly organized on a regular basis.

My daughter was right. At the time of her statement, I absolutely did not look like someone who writes about organization (that's not what she said, but it's *so* what I heard!) But, after my initial response, I needed to remind myself of a couple of things I already knew.

First, a temporary overabundance of piles does not mean I've fallen into utter, hopeless disorganization. And, second, the fact that this happens at my house from time to time is precisely why I write about this.

I'm not flawlessly organized. My house is not perfect 24-7 (far from it). My systems, which keep me organized most of the time, get overwhelmed sometimes.

And there's a good reason for that. *I* get overwhelmed sometimes and, since my systems are an extension of my styles (which are an extension of me), when I get overwhelmed, they do, too. Sometimes, it's simply a matter of re-sasserting control over my belongings. Sometimes, it's a matter of rethinking the systems. Either way, I need more than a pinch of a magic ingredient that has little to do with me, my styles or my systems.

Time.

I write about this because I get it. I know how hard it is to keep things together all the time. I'm not writing to lecture from on high but, rather, to share what I've learned in the hopes it will help you, your kids, your spouse or your seemingly hopelessly disorganized best friend. Together, we'll figure this out, stumble, acquire, declutter, figure it out again and make progress.

It's a process and, for some of us, it involves piles.

True Confession #11: No matter how much I try to keep up with it, all the house stuff drops to the bottom of the list during the week.

LATELY, my weekends have been busy. Mostly, they've been busy with good things, but they've been busy nevertheless. Blocking out a Saturday here, a Sunday afternoon there and occasionally, traveling one or more days during the week has begun to take its toll and has brought me to a clear realization.

I need Saturdays.

On Saturdays, my priorities shift. Rather than being crammed into the nooks and crannies of the day as they are during the week, house stuff and writing stuff top the list on Saturdays. My students, with few exceptions, stop sending emails sometime Friday afternoon and resume sometime Sunday, making it easy to step away from work emails and grading. My family is home and the house isn't always quiet, making it the right time to do tasks like clutter-busting and re-organizing.

Without my Saturdays, things fall apart rather quickly. While I can pick up as I go or toss a load of laundry in on a weekday, really digging in to the things I want to do around the house just doesn't happen.

This Saturday, for the first time in nearly a month, I will have time at home. While there will be some grading to do, I'm ready to dig into the piles that have popped up around my house during the weeks when my Saturdays were spoken for.

I can't wait to dig in.

True Confession #12: Organizing makes my short list of fun things to do when I have a day off.

NO, that's not sarcasm, which is probably why I spend so much time writing about this stuff. And, as I've said before, the organizing and the writing feed each other. When I write about my problem areas in a blog post here, I get motivated to wave my magic organizing wand (so to speak) and make them disappear.

Unfortunately, there is no magic organizing wand. It's all good ideas (and some bad ones) and elbow grease. And time — the most elusive ingredient of all.

After last week's blog post, I made it a point to take the time to properly organize the student papers that were littering my dining room table. I had them stacked by class but, because of the way I'd collected the assignments, some of the piles had multiple assignments in them. Writing last week's post nudged me to grab three card stock filing bins (green, blue and yellow, for those of you color-coding at home), separate the papers by assignment and turn the stacks and piles into neatly (color-coded) paper-clipped stacks all contained within one file per class. I'd been putting off doing this because I'd had my blinders on, careening forward and "accomplishing things" instead of stopping and taking the time to put things in an order that would reduce my stress.

Just me?

The thing is, I really enjoy *organizing*. I'm not wild about cleaning (unless it's cleaning a newly cleared space) or cooking, but organizing? Lemme at it!

Last Sunday, I had papers to grade so, of course, I

cleared off the counter in my office. (Did I mention that organizing is also a procrastination technique of mine?) Since then, every time I've walked into the office, my eyes light on that newly cleared space and I smile. There is still work to be done as well as projects I'm eyeing up in other parts of the house, but that space makes me happy *and* more likely to spend time in my office.

When we get busy, it's easy to put off organizing. We run from one thing on our to-do lists to the next, claiming we don't have time to stop and sort. But, if you're like me, when you finally *make* the time to do just that, the act of taking stock and putting things into order can be just the stress relief we need. Sorting all those papers on my dining room didn't reduce the number of papers I had to grade, but it allowed me to get a better idea of what was actually there and corral what looked like haphazard piles. Suddenly, I was in charge, running the task instead of the task running me.

Over my upcoming break, I hope to express my gratitude in multiple ways. One of them will be getting rid of outdated and excess things so I can truly enjoy what I have. I won't get to tackle all my problem areas, but I have a few spots I want to dig into. I gave my students the assignment of savoring something over their break and I can't think of a better way to savor what matters than to remove all the stuff that gets in the way of my enjoying it — or noticing it — in the first place.

True confession #13: I leave my browser tabs open.

LOTS OF THEM. All the time. On multiple devices.

Can you say "I need to see it?"

Since I use my laptop in class, this has shocked more than one of my students. A few have even offered to "clean up" my desktop for me. Clearly they don't understand that their idea of cleaning up my laptop would *not* be helpful. Hide my tabs??

Still, I'm embarrassed. I can't help feeling as though it somehow makes me look less professional.

So, when I took my MacBook into the Apple store because it was having power issues, I asked one of the technicians about this habit, and whether or not it was the cause of the battery issues. He shook his head (in a good way) and assured me it wasn't a problem. "That's what this machine was designed for," he said.

That was all I needed to hear. I mean, I already loved my MacBook and now someone who knew what he was talking about was telling me it was designed for my *I need to see it* style?

Music to my ears!

And so now, when one of my students is horrified by all of my open browser tabs and/or the collection of colored folders on my MacBook desktop, I remember that technician at the Apple store. I know my plan doesn't work for everyone, but it doesn't have to. From time to time, if it's not working for me, I need to go in and see which tabs need to be closed but, otherwise, it's my style and I'm sticking to it.

True Confession #14: I love stationery.

THIS IS something that's been true ever since I was a little girl. We'd go to a five and ten or a variety store (yes, I'm *that* old!) and I would spend as much time as I could wandering the aisles filled with notebooks and various kinds of paper. I still remember the pink notebook paper I got to fill my flowered binder in elementary school (fourth grade, if memory serves) and how I saved it for special assignments.

To this day, I have a collection of notebooks waiting to be pressed into service (because one needs a notebook that is *just right* for the task at hand), a collection of file folders in various colors, patterns, materials (traditional card stock vs. acetate/plastic) and sizes, and enough Post-it Notes to paper my office. Granted, it's a small office, but that's still a lot of sticky notes.

I also match my writing implements to the task for which I'm using them. But that's another post.

So, when KnockKnockStuff.com had its Black Friday (or was it Cyber Monday?) sale, of course I needed to add to my collection. I was running out of pages on the tablet I use to create the week-at-a-glance sheet that travels between work and home, linking my commitments in both places, so re-ordering those was a no-brainer. While I was there, I found a daily to-do page I liked and added that to my cart as well. Sure, I could use a blank sheet of paper, or the back of my week-at-a-glance page but, *I need to see it* person that I am, the combination of eye-catching and priority-based (breaking up the longer list into smaller lists based on urgency) was too good to pass up.

Oh, and did I mention that it sticks to stuff? Like, say, the back of my weekly list?

You don't have to be Santa for lists to be a big part of

your life, especially during the holidays. And, while any piece of paper (or notebook) will do in a pinch, having a list that's very visible (and maybe even prioritized) can be just the ticket to bringing a little bit of organization to a busy, somewhat overwhelming time of year.

And, who knows? Maybe if you leave him some cookies, Santa will add that just-right notepad or notebook to your stocking -- the one that works for your style. And if the cookies are just right, maybe all the items will already be checked off.

Now that would be a gift indeed.

True Confession #15: I'm a beat-the-clock kind of organizer.

I *DON'T* MEAN that I quickly scramble to put things away when company's coming (although that does sometimes happen). Instead, what I mean is that I've learned to use small pockets of time to my advantage. While this doesn't work well for major projects, it's great for making progress in smaller ones. In fifteen minutes or less I can zap a pile, return homeless items to their homes, make the bed, put away a load of laundry....

You get the idea.

Sometimes, these pockets of time arise between activities. Other times, they're a way of making a dent in an otherwise daunting task like cleaning the basement or overhauling a closet. These short bursts can be an organizing session unto themselves, or they can be the start of something more, nudging me to complete a task I expected only to start. Either way, they often lead me to replace clutter with clear space which is the ultimate prize in the organizing game.

Admittedly, not everything in life can be accomplished in fifteen minutes or less; some tasks call for a longer commitment. But while I wait for that elusive block of time to arrive, it's nice to know I can chip away at tasks a little at a time.

And end up with clear space to boot.

True Confession #16: I love planners.

I'VE READ that we should have only one planner — a master planner, in which we keep track of everything. I tried that. And, while it worked (sort of) when my daughter was small and I was working a traditional job and keeping traditional hours, it wasn't a perfect fit.

When I retired from my job as a school counselor, I rethought the single planner approach. These days, I keep separate planners for work and home, as well as a writing planner in which I keep track of goals, submissions and other writerly things. I also create a week-at-a-glance sheet every week after consulting with my family to make sure I'm up to date on appointments that don't involve me (we do this over dinner on Friday nights). In a pinch, I use the calendar on my phone, but only when I need to note an appointment and don't have my planner with me. My *I need to see it* personal style means that old school (paper and pencil) works way better for me than electronic.

Clearly, I'm about as far-removed from a single planner person as you can get and, while I'm sure that sounds unwieldy to many people, it works for me. I'm also very picky about my planners and can take a long time choosing one that's just right. There are features I *must* have, features I'd like to have and a price point I try not to go past.

As you read through the rest of this post, think about (and maybe even jot down) the features that are *needs* and *wants* for your style. The planner I'm virtually flipping through (Author Journey: Weekly Planner & Success Guide by Demi Stevens and Laurie J. Edwards) might be the one for you, or it might not but, since it has a lot to offer, it's a great way to dissect a planner and break down the things we need as we choose the ones that work for us.

The cover: Okay, you can't judge a book (especially a planner) by its cover...but I do. The pristine inside of a planner is going to go from blank to overwhelming before you can say New Year's resolution, so I want the outside of my planner to evoke calm, and this one does.

The front matter: Honestly, I never really thought about front matter — I like space to jot notes, but beyond that, I never really considered the pages that come before the calendar pages. Laurie and Demi thought about it, though, and used the front of the book to wed the year that's ending to the one that's just beginning, allowing space for the user to move from where she was and is to where she wants to go. These are the kinds of things I use the margins of my writer planner for but, in this planner, there's dedicated space for these considerations.

The layout. When I'm shopping for my school planner, any calendar that doesn't have both a month- at-a-glance and a week-at-a-glance goes right back on the shelf. (I use just month-at-a-glance for my personal and writing calendars). This planner goes one better, including year-at-a-glance in the front matter, as well as my necessary views (monthly, weekly). The margins in the monthly view allow dedicated space for writing the year's goals, while the weekly view includes to-do list space, monthly goal space, and room for jotting down other things of importance as well. There's also a monthly overview at the end of each month to review where you've been before you decide where you want to go. And at the space for notes? Lots of it.

Whether we're looking for planners, or anything else, for that matter, it's always nice when the item we find not only meets our needs and wants (and fits our styles), but also provides things we didn't realize we needed and/or wanted in the first place. One of the reasons I abandoned the single-planner approach was the sheer size of the planner I needed in order to keep track of *everything*, but this planner has me thinking it'd be awfully nice to have just one place to go. Or, as the authors say in their intro, "Having a place to keep all this information helps us focus on the things that matter."

What do you want in your planner?

True Confession #17: I'm a little bit *I love stuff*.

WHEN I INTRODUCE the styles at meetings and conferences and/or when people take the styles quiz, almost inevitably, someone asks if they can be all of them. My response is that, while it seems that way at first, for most of us, one predominant personal style and one predominant organizational style emerge.

That doesn't mean, however, that traces of other styles don't linger, influencing the way we do things. The *I love to be busy* style is a great example. Many people *don't* love to be busy, but have had busyness thrust upon them by the multiple roles they play. For them, successful organizing and planning might very well mean taking strategies for the *I love to be busy* personal style into account, making it almost a secondary style choice.

Though my primary styles are *I need to see it* (personal) and *drop and run* (organizational), I can feel my *I love stuff* tendencies arise when I'm decluttering a space. I can be ruthless about many things, but I keep arguably more than my fair share of sentimental mementos. It's not the *thing* I want as much as what it evokes— memories of times and places past. While I've gotten a lot better at getting rid of things I was saving only because I *should* save them, there are plenty of extras that survive the purge.

Another time I can feel my *I love stuff* tendencies rising up and clamoring to be heard is when I wander through the aisles at The Container Store or even my local Target. I want it all! Okay, maybe not *all* of it, but I'm intrigued by the sheer variety and quantity of organizers that are available. Again, I've made progress in that I only take home what I truly think I will use, but my basement is a testament to the fact that it hasn't always been that way (see True Confession #1), and that I should always "shop" there before heading out to buy new things.

When I think about it, the connection between my primary *I need to see it* personal style and my secondary *I love stuff* tendencies is clear. It's a need for the visual. The same part of me that responds to visual cues is emotionally cued by certain objects and drawn in by the visual appeal of pretty things. Knowing this, I can be more analytical about the choices I make, whether it's deciding what to keep and what to toss or when to buy and when to pass.

In the end, which style prevails? For me, my *I need to see **it*** style steers the ship and runs the show. It's more consistent than my *I love stuff* tendencies and, when pressed into service, it helps me to organize sustainably. In the end, my *I need to see it* style and its first runner-up work together so that I'm organized in a way that consistently works for me, while making things look pretty in the process.

True Confession #18: I have one-more-thing-itis.

FOR A LONG TIME, I made a resolution every January and on many Ash Wednesdays to be on time. There are a few things in life I'm never late for (work, massage appointments) but, much of the time, I am running anywhere from two to ten minutes behind. The cause of this is clear and consistent.

I have one-more-thing-itis — a terrible case of believing that I can fit in just "one more thing." Whether it's one more task, one more sentence, or one more time hitting the snooze button, I prove myself wrong much of the time, discovering only when it's too late that I really did *not* have time for one more.

When I try to do this before leaving the house, I inevitably end up late to wherever I'm going. When I try to do this before I start dinner, we end up eating dinner later than planned. When I try to do this before winding down/going to bed, I end up not getting enough sleep.

In a way, it's a very optimistic outlook (I'm sure I can squeeze in one more thing!) and it can even seem efficient, as though I'm using my time wisely by filling all my nooks and crannies of time with items from my to-do list. But, in the end, I don't end up being very efficient at all. Instead, I end up hungry, sleepy and late and I often inconvenience others as well.

I've been aware of this problem for quite some time; I've even come up with ways to work on it. I'm improving but I still have a way to go.

I've begun to consider what might be at the root of this issue. *Why* do I always think I can fit in one more thing? Sometimes, as noted above, it's optimism. Other times, it's denial ("It really won't take me that long to get there") or dread ("I don't want to have this hanging over my head, so I want to finish it now"). In the end, it's a time management problem that creates another time management problem.

As with any habit, the desire to change has to precede the change itself. Most of the time, especially when the thing I'm going to is as interesting as (or even better than) the thing I'm coming from, that desire is there. It's in those other moments, the ones where I just hate to stop what I'm doing, that the habit digs its heels in, becoming entrenched.

As I type this now, I have one eye on the clock, knowing my alarm is going to go off in five minutes so I can get ready to go to church.

Will I stop? Or will I shave five minutes off the time I allotted for church. I'm sure I can get one more thing in....

True Confession #19: I want what I want because I know what I need.

FOR THE PAST FEW WEEKS, I've been trying to figure out how to create a true-to-my-styles, unobtrusive drop spot for my school folders. While the fact that it's a drop spot (or it will be) makes it a perfect fit for my *drop and run* organizational style, the idea of unobtrusive is a challenge for my *I need to see it* personal style.

I've been at this long enough to have learned that when I know what I want the end result to be, but I'm not sure how to get there, I need to be patient. Turning all the relevant questions over in my mind allows me to consider all the possibilities until one snaps into place.

And it almost always does.

When I shared my dilemma with my husband, he immediately suggested my office, which sounds perfectly logical coming from someone with an *I know I put it somewhere* organizational style, but fails both the *drop and run* and *I need to see it* tests. My office is as far from the door I use to enter the house as it could possibly be, making that location neither accessible nor visible. While my drop spot needs to be somewhat tucked away so things don't look cluttered, it also needs to be close to where I pack up (and drop) my supplies each day.

Long story short, I determined a potential location on Saturday and on Sunday, I suddenly knew exactly which tool I needed to make things work. As I write this, I'm awaiting its arrival, looking forward to seeing how it works. I suspect I'll end up taking apart what's already there and relocating some of it, but that's not such a bad idea. The space I've identified is one of those where the things that live there landed there and just stayed. Rethinking their location and giving them intentional homes might be a bonus I hadn't considered when I started thinking about my drop spot.

One of the benefits of learning how to work with our styles is that we get good at figuring out what we need to make a space work. I've reached the point where I know precisely what I want and what I don't want because I know my styles. While it might take me a little bit of brainstorming before that lighting bolt answer arrives, once that happens, I usually arrive at a long-term solution that everyone can live with. I rarely waste money on tools that don't work and I often improve the spaces surrounding the target area as well.

When it comes to organizing by STYLE, I've found that practice does make perfect — or at least it provides a shortcut to easy upkeep.

True Confession #20: I love simple solutions.

LAST WEEK, after thinking about it for a while and talking about it here, I created my drop spot -- just a simple felt tray. Unobtrusive, it has no bells and whistles. It's not perfect (it might be better if it were slightly wider), but it works. Creating the new habit of using it came naturally, which tells me it's the right tool in the right place.

Sometimes, the simplest solution is the answer.

A week or so ago, I stumbled upon another simple solution. When I (finally) sit down to write, my loudest distractions are internal — go do this, don't forget that, are you sure that's the best way to say that? While that last one can only be tackled with enough time spent writing, the first can be easily dispensed with by taking a moment to jot them down and let them go. For this purpose, I keep a notepad beside my computer so I can do just that. Or, if I want to do a little on-the-fly advance planning, I can use two sticky notes instead: one for tasks I want to complete during the week and one for things I hope to get to on the weekend. (My *I need to see it* personal style dictates that they be different colors, of course). I can then stick them right inside my planner or on my weekly summary until each task finds a spot on my schedule.

So often, we make organizing harder than it has to be. The next time you're confronted with an organizational challenge, don't just ask yourself the best way to do solve it; in addition, ask yourself the easiest way. Much of the time, the answer to both questions is exactly the same, leaving us with more time at our disposal to tackle life's really tough challenges.

True confession #21: I'm here 24-7 and my house still isn't completely organized. (A pandemic post)

I THOUGHT for sure that when we were all required to stay home and socially distance ourselves that it might finally happen. I might tackle all the piles, sort through all the stuff and create clear space as far as the eye could see.

In the past eleven days, I have left the house only once — to go to the grocery store. Meanwhile, back at our small Cape Cod, organizing to-dos remain on the list. The dining room table has been cleared of its egregious piles (because my daughter is using it for her Zoom sessions) and only a few scattered items of mine remain. I clear my desk every night, the mail pile has shrunk, and we spent three hours cleaning a section of the basement last weekend, but perfect organization has not yet become a reality.

Maybe I need eleven more days? Eleven days without teaching responsibilities that include learning how to use online tools?

While that would help, I'm pretty sure that still wouldn't do it. And I'm pretty sure I'm looking at this wrong, too. Only a few scattered items of mine remain on the dining room table, I clear my desk (which was a haven for piles — and a dusty one at that — only a few months ago) every night, the mail pile has shrunk (and needs about ten more minutes of dedicated time to disappear entirely), and we spent three hours cleaning a section of the basement last weekend and generating more trash than we can legally put out in a week.

That's progress.

Sure, I have a list of organizing projects — probably

longer than the list of things I've accomplished — but that's how life works. There is always something to do, and that's as true of organizing as it is of anything else. And, if I'm honest, most of those projects haven't made it out of my head and onto my list yet because I'm occupied with all the changes our current circumstances bring.

So, for now, I'll focus on what I *have* done, even as the things I *haven't* done seem to scream at me as I walk past. The ones that scream most loudly (or are suggested by someone else, like our basement, which was my husband's idea) will make it to the list (first) and, eventually, to completion.

Or, more accurately, disappearance. But it always has been, and remains, a process.

No matter how many hours I spend in the house.

**True Confession #22: My drop-and-run systems
are often just piles in disguise.**

A COUPLE OF WEEKS AGO, I was looking for a place
to store my daughter's gluten-free stash without doing a
major kitchen storage overhaul. My eyes lit on the bins
underneath my mail counter, two of which were only
partially full (room to grow), so I reached into the middle
one, pulled out a pile of magazines and voilà! Problem
solved.

Except now I have a pile of homeless (and probably
outdated) magazines.

For now, this pile is on the steps leading to the second
floor of our house. Last weekend, I was good at picking up a
new magazine every time — okay, many times — when I
passed the piles but, as the week got busy, the pile got
neglected.

I could just add it to one of the (many) other piles of
reading materials I have but I keep holding out hope that its
current location will catch my *I need to see it* eye so that I
solve the problem rather than compounding it.

Getting back to my original confession, the concept of
piles in disguise is not entirely bad. After all, when you
think about it, most organizing systems for papers are organized piles. Binders. File cabinets. In/out boxes.

My magazine bin.

The trick is to keep the pile organized in whatever way
works for your styles. I have one bin that is all catalogs so
that when I get the mail, every catalog either goes there or
gets recycled immediately (**Don't put it *down*, put it
away**). When I'm looking for a catalog, I look in the bin
(the home for catalogs) and when it gets full, it's time to go

through the catalogs and get rid of duplicates (two from the same company) and anything outdated. This is a pile in disguise (the bin being its disguise) but, since it's not haphazard, it's also an organized pile. The bin contains everything, matches its neighbors and leaves things looking better than a random pile of magazines would.

As for the pile sitting on my steps? Now a random pile, it *was* an organized pile before I sacrificed my bin for the greater good. How was it not random in the bin? Only certain magazines got slipped into that bin so that if I were looking for one of those issues, I'd know where to find it.

As I've mentioned before, this blog is therapeutic in that writing about what I need to do often gives me the nudge I need to do the thing I wrote about. With some time off next week, maybe I'll tackle that pile and not only get rid of it, but read its contents. Or maybe tonight I should just take the whole thing back in the family room and get rid of whatever's in there that I know I won't read anyway, assuming those items actually exist. Either of those would be progress.

Stay tuned.

True Confession #23: Sometimes, I use a binder.

IT'S RARE. In fact, it almost feels *wrong*. I've spent so much time railing against doing things the usual way that choosing a standard tool makes me feel like a traitor to STYLE.

But a week or so ago, there I was, searching my stockpile for a just-right binder. The stack of printouts from my online course needed to go somewhere and, since I was pretty sure I'd want to reference them, that somewhere needed to keep them organized and accessible.

A binder was, in this case, the just right tool — the Goldilocks to my burgeoning paper pile.

So, stylish binder in hand (none of those standard-issue solid color binders for this *I need to see it* girl), I sat down with my stack of papers, my three-hole punch, and my sticky tabs and I did one of my favorite things.

I made order out of chaos.

I've written a lot about making the break from traditional tools, but I've also written a lot about choosing the right container for the job. In this case, I needed to keep the papers in order, so a file folder or accordion file didn't make sense. I needed to be able to flip through them easily, take them out and put them back again, and store them neatly in between uses before setting them aside until next fall.

I needed a binder.

While I don't care for binders for everyday use, I do like them (especially if they're eye-catching) for reference materials that can — and do — stay out of sight until needed. They work better for my *I need to see it* personal style than file cabinets because once I open the binder, things are visible and, if I've organized them correctly in the first place, they are accessible as well.

Organizing by STYLE doesn't mean we'll *never* use standard tools — it just means we won't default to them. Though I've moved away from binders and file cabinets, there are times when I choose them because they are the right tool for me and for the job — something that is at the heart of organizing by STYLE. In addition, when we choose to use a standard tool, we can personalize it. My binder is eye-catching (to go with my *I need to see it* personal style) and, when I add my sticky tabs to the pages, I can see what's where and flip through the pages easily. Down the road, I might also add a clip to the front, or a divider with pockets but, for now, my binder is working quite well.

I'm as surprised as you are.

True Confession #24: I like to do things my way. (Another pandemic post)

EVERYONE WHO KNOWS ME, along with anyone who reads this blog on a regular basis is laughing at the understatement embodied in that sentence.

I'm not inflexible. I just know what I like.

But this post isn't about me. It's about your kids.

As we all spend lots of — ahem — *quality time* together, melding home and school and every possession, plaything, or educational material into one big, overwhelming, previously organized space, we may be struggling to keep it — I mean things — together. And we all know what we like.

And it's probably not happening.

Believe it or not, kids have organizing styles too. Sometimes they match ours, sometimes they don't. But a surefire way to keep your kids from organizing their stuff is to disregard their styles and do it yourself (a.k.a. according to your styles) because it's easier. It might be easier (and faster) but, rather than teaching them how to organize, it's teaching them that if they leave things disorganized for long enough, someone else will come along behind them and organize it for them.

Sometimes, after the organizing angel has worked her magic (although at my house, the angel is more likely to moonlight as a dad), the children in question have the nerve — no, the *gall!* — to complain about how it was done.

Can you believe that?

What looks like a serious case of entitlement is often a difference in styles. I'm not promising you that if you ask your children what their styles are that they will magically fall in line and put away every last possession, plaything, and educational material without being asked. But I am suggesting that you ask them what might work for them.

Maybe even give them this very scientific quiz I made up (http://bit.ly/2HOTYzy).

Teaching our kids to organize most often begins with modeling the strategies that come naturally to us. Sometimes, our kids will adopt those same strategies and develop organizing systems that look like ours and, when it comes time to clean up at the end of the day, they will do so to our satisfaction.

Others will not but, when we offer them alternatives, they might develop their own strategies and systems. They might even like the responsibility of caring for their own things when they can do it their way. Even better, it's possible that they've learned a thing or two from all those things that didn't work. With a little encouragement and a lot of flexibility, we can help them develop a life skill while they're still living at home where we can appreciate it.

Adults don't have the market cornered on wanting to do things our way. Honoring your child's styles can, in the end, make both of you happy.

After all, everyone loves a little ownership.

True Confession #25: Tonight, instead of writing this blog, I mixed myself a drink and indulged in a Zoom happy hour with friends.

WHAT DOES this have to do with organization?

Not a thing. But it has a lot to do with time management and self-care. I'd spent the whole day on school stuff — meetings, emails, grading — and had gone back to my desk after dinner to finish a set of papers. More papers — and planning — loomed, as did this blog post.

Take a break?

No better time.

I'm not complaining. I love my job and I love writing these posts. Though I prefer to do both during the daylight hours, that's not always how it plays out, mostly because I have a hard time stepping away. Sometimes I need an excuse, but even when one shows up in my inbox, I can be a little dense.

Today was (fortunately) not one of those days.

Powering through is sometimes what we need but, more often, it isn't. If the fuse is lit and we're on fire to finish something, powering through is the way to go. But when our minds and bodies are telling us otherwise, listening is the smart thing to do.

Today was a difficult day — nothing major, just one of those days — but tomorrow will be better because I took care of myself tonight.

Take care of you. There's no better investment.

True Confession #26: Sometimes, it pays to be a packrat.

ON MONDAY NIGHT, (day 41 of self-imposed exile, for those of you keeping score at home), I pulled the lid off my signature scent (a fancy way of saying my only bottle of perfume) and the nozzle came off with it. Securely wedged inside, it wouldn't budge, leaving me with a nearly full bottle and no way to spray it. It was late, so I went to bed, saddened at the thought of wasting all of that perfume.

The next morning, I got up and took another look. Nope — no miracles. Still inextricably wedged inside. I twisted the little strip of gold that remained at the top of the perfume bottle and the spray mechanism came loose.

Okay, good. I wouldn't have to waste the perfume. But where was I going to pour it? My mom used to have one of those vanity trays with the glass bottles for various fragrances, but those were long gone.

Wait.

I pulled open the top drawer of my dresser and there it was.

The old bottle.

There was only whisper of liquid left, but the most important part remained. I quickly pulled off the lid (gently this time), unscrewed the spray mechanism and, I'm embarrassed to say, got ready to pour.

Yeah, there was an easier way. I swapped the mechanisms and returned the old bottle to the drawer, exceedingly happy about a very simple thing.

When I saved that bottle, I had no really good reason. A faint aroma still lingered, so I tucked it in my dresser drawer as a sort of glass sachet.

Yeah. No good reason to keep it and pretty much every

professional organizer on the planet would tell me to toss it. But I kept it because I wanted to and now I'm really glad I did.

Sometimes, we save things for a good reason. Other times, we just want to. We can't keep everything we've ever owned but, despite the fact that something borrowed should always be returned, something old doesn't always need to end up in the trash. (When it comes to something blue, I'll let you decide).

Has an all-but-empty perfume bottle led me to contradict **L**et it Go! (The L in STYLE)? Quite the opposite, actually. **L**et it Go! has always been about letting go of things on your own terms. If something has meaning or use and you have room for it, keep it. If its time has passed or it's not worth the space it will take up, perhaps it is time for it to exit your home, whether via donation, yard sale or — dare I say it? — the trash.

Now that I think of it, I'm not sure why I tucked that old bottle back in the drawer. Habit, I guess. Perhaps it's time to go back upstairs and apply my own rules. Its usefulness has passed (it consists of a non-working mechanism atop an all-but-empty bottle of perfume) and, if no further fragrance lingers, there's really no reason to keep it. And getting rid of something old makes way for something new or, perhaps even better, yields clear space.

But that's another post.

True confession #27: I am sometimes free flow and sometimes structured.

EVERYONE HAS a Type A organizer friend who is seemingly always on it. She sets a goal, establishes a routine and rarely deviates from it.

Or maybe that she is a he — I've just described my husband.

Me? I'm mood-driven. I make lists and I get to the things that are on them, but I'm also likely to take a detour (or two) along the way. Is this a bad thing?

Not always. When I try to force myself to chip away at my to-do list, but am actually interested in doing something else, I tend to procrastinate and do neither. Consequently, I've learned that caving in and doing the task I want to be doing (within reason) while I have the energy to do it is sometimes a good call. Sometimes, this choice even gives me a wave of energy I can ride from the beginning of the task to its completion.

Score one for free flow.

Notice, please, that I'm comparing two tasks, like washing the dishes when I should be writing a blog post (okay, that's just procrastination) or cleaning out a drawer when I should be grading papers (too close to call). I'm *not* talking about binge-watching *The Marvelous Mrs. Maisel* when I should be doing something productive — that's an entirely different post.

Right now, I'm in a nose-to-the-grindstone kind of week. I have a deadline for grading papers and calculating grades, and so I have no real option to go off-topic. (This, of course, only makes me want to go off-topic even more). At times like these, I often segment my day to get a sense of completion, breaking the day up into 30-60 minute segments in order to stay on task, assigning a task to each time block in order to get things done.

Score one for structured.

I've tried to be like this all the time — to emulate my Type A organizer friends who follow the rules and check things off their lists, but it's just not my style. Though slipping from free-flow to structured and back again doesn't seem logical, it works for me. It gives me the best of both worlds, allowing me to tackle things when I'm in the right frame of mind to do them well and to put my nose to the grindstone when I need to.

And, in the end, isn't the point just to get things done?

True Confession #28: My basement could pass for an outpost of The Container Store.

I'D LIKE to say it all started when I retired and the leftovers from the organizer giveaways I did with my students made their way into my basement.

I'd like to say that, but I don't think it's entirely true. Bringing all of those things home simply put my existing container supply over the top. And my stint as a Thirty-One Gifts consultant did not make the piles any smaller.

We have lived in our house (a three-bedroom Cape Cod) for almost 26 years. Many of the spaces in the house have changed over time, keeping pace with the life changes that have occurred. A guest room became a nursery, then a bedroom whose decor and storage grew and changed with its occupant. A downstairs bedroom became an office, then a catch-all space, then a playroom, and, finally, a family room. A side porch became an office.

Not only did the different versions of each of the rooms necessitate its own unique storage, but tastes changed over time as well. Plastic bins hidden behind closet doors didn't make the cut when storage came out of the closet and into the living space. Storage for toddler toys didn't do the trick for tween collections or the electronics that followed. And, this afternoon, the young adult who inhabits what was once the nursery spent several hours trying to figure out where her college furniture will go when we bring it home in a few days.

Meanwhile, the usable castoffs have taken up residence — and space — in my basement. Bins of various sizes and colors, some with lids, some without, are stacked in a corner of my basement. A variety of leftover paper storage, cloth bins and various purses and tote bags inhabit other areas.

The good news is that if we ever need storage for, well, *anything*, we know just where to look. And it's free. Kinda.

The bad news is that it's most likely more than we will ever need. But, since it's not really taking up enough space to be bothersome, there it all stays.

The college graduate living upstairs will likely take some of it with her when she moves into an apartment of her own -- or at least that's my current excuse for leaving it all as is. She's also going through a sell-the-old-stuff-online phase that may allow me to thin the collection a bit.

At some point, I'll have had enough and I'll sort through everything (again) and decide what to keep, what to sell, and what to donate. But, until we can actually get the boxes of donations that are already down there out of the house, it feels futile. And, as is often the case, I'm sure that I'll need exactly the container I donated right after I give it away.

So for now, there it all sits, gathering dust and waiting to be useful. My own little storage supply outpost, ready to corral some clutter.

True Confession #29: I am inspired by other people's organizational efforts.

LAST WEEKEND, we moved my daughter out of college housing for the last time. As a senior, her housing was a literal *house* with three other girls. Four girls, five bedrooms, two bathrooms, a living room, eat-in kitchen and finished space that used to be a garage, along with a small back porch and a yard the university took care of for them. It was basically a great little starter house with fewer responsibilities, and she only got to live there for a little over a semester. I felt really cheated for her.

She had a lot of fun putting her room together and adapting to living in a house instead of a dorm, and she had the belongings to prove it. She'd gone up once after spring break to bring some things home and had found out on the way home that she wouldn't be returning to face-to-face classes this semester.

And so, on the designated day in May at the designated hour (COVID-19 had led to staggered move-out times, with no overlapping between roommates), we arrived to pick up everything the university had already packed up. With the house to ourselves, we did a little sorting through the boxes in the common rooms, a little culling of the boxes in her room and managed to fit everything into the backs of our two cars. She got to do a masked visit with a few friends in other houses who had the same move-out time that she did and before we left, she and I spent a little time sitting in her living room processing it all. In the end, it was a low-drama move out and we didn't have to leave anything of substance behind except memories.

Then we got home, and the real adventure began.

She had started readying her bedroom prior to the move

out, and the piles of things to be sold or donated had already begun to form. Now, they are larger.

She is methodical in her work, and thorough, putting her styles to work and consulting with me when she needs a second opinion. And while the piles are setting my teeth on edge a bit, the brainstorming, combined with my first summer off in several years, is nudging me to do some re-organizing and re-configuring of my own. On Saturday night, I appropriated a cast-off drawer unit of hers and re-did a section of my office. Things are still a little chaotic because what was a good move aesthetically triggered some organizational challenges I've yet to resolve.

It's a process.

I'm trying to be patient with the piles, knowing that they are temporary, and part of a larger process. She has her own styles and her own plan of attack and she's made enormous progress in a short time. Meanwhile, I love being her assistant/consultant as she transforms her room into a tran-sitional living space and inspires me to make some changes of my own.

What inspires you to organize?

True confession #30: There are both weak spots and cracks in my organizational systems.

AFTER MORE THAN a decade of reading about organization, formulating my Organizing by STYLE philosophy, and putting that philosophy to work, I've repaired all the gaping holes in my organizational system. I can't say my house is clutter-free, or that my system is perfect, but it has definitely improved.

Still, I'm left with weak spots and cracks. A weak spot is (by my definition) something that kind of works but isn't really a long-term solution. Sometimes, the weakness is easily identifiable (wrong container, wrong spot, wrong size) but, until the weak spot becomes a tear or a crack, or until I find a replacement container/spot/accommodation, it'll do.

Cracks are bigger, more time sensitive, and more prone to actually giving way. Like a stack of papers that could topple over at any moment, cracks are systems that could fall apart without warning. The sooner they are addressed, the better.

I hope it's obvious that what I'm talking about here isn't literal weak spots or cracks, but rather flaws and problem spots that need to be addressed. Sometimes, a trail of clutter leads us to them or sometimes they self-destruct under the weight of a responsibility they weren't designed to handle.

Take my mail counter, for example. Regular readers know it was a weak spot (and sometimes a crack) for *years* as I tried one inadequate solution after another. Its conspicuous location made it a source of not just clutter but embarrassment as well until, eventually, I found the right tools and created a system that works.

Last weekend, I attacked another weak spot — my

bedroom closet. The floor was littered with boxes that held out-of-season shoes that had no other home. The hanging rods worked but, upon closer inspection, when was the last time I'd worn *anything* hanging on the rod that was least accessible?

Hmm.

Long story short, the clothes are in a donation pile, the rod has been removed and a small, cheap shelf unit (thank you, Target) now sits where the clothes were hanging, providing a home for all those formerly homeless shoes. Nearly every pair of shoes I own is now visible or in a clearly labeled box (an *I need to see it* victory!). There's one remaining bin of casual sandals that's in limbo. If they get worn this season, they'll earn a spot on a shelf. If not, they'll go into the donation box, too.

Why did I go so long accepting the fact that I was unable to see the floor of my closet? It was a weak spot. Workable enough to suffice (I could access everything — kinda), it didn't require my immediate attention. But, once it got my immediate attention, it inspired me to tackle other clutter in my bedroom as well — mostly because, as with most organizing projects, things got worse before they got better. Now, not only does the closet look better, so do a few other spaces in the room.

Weak spots often hide in plain sight. That pile of clothes that's been on the chair for so long, you no longer see it. The stack of papers that has made itself at home on the dining room table. The almost-right container in the sort of right location that holds things you don't know where to put.

Organizing is a dynamic process that needs to be flexible enough to adjust to the constant flow of "stuff" into and out of our homes. As life changes, our systems have to change, too, but, if we know what our styles are and how they work, those changes are more of a pivot than an all-out makeover. If we tackle the weak spots while they're still just that, we can save ourselves the headache of repairing a crack that has given way.

And, perhaps best of all, we can create beautiful, coveted clear space in the process.

True Confession #31: I cannot imagine that I will ever get to inbox zero.

LATELY, I've been working on reducing the embarrassingly high number of emails in my inboxes at work and at home. I've also been working on being more intentional in my consumption of the news and in my use of social media, as both have a tendency to impact my mood and, therefore, my actions.

The other day, as I was working, emails were coming in, as they usually do. I've gotten pretty good at glancing quickly at the sender and then getting back to work, often deleting the incoming mail before it hits my inbox.

On that particular day, though, I became more aware of my reaction to the incoming mail. I caught myself making a face when a newsletter I'd subscribed to quite some time ago came across the screen.

Clearly, I was never going to read that newsletter — or the rest of the collection taking up space in my inbox — but instead of that being problematic, it sparked a plan.

First of all, I did a search for all those newsletters (Wow! More than 50!), unsubscribed, and deleted them. Very freeing.

Then, I decided that might be the foundation of a plan that could help not only my inbox, but my mood as well. I get tons of junk in my inbox, and most of it registers as neutral or nuisance. How much was that affecting me? And why should I be letting anything into my inbox on a regular basis if it doesn't make me smile when I see it there?

So, I decided that any time I got an email that triggered a negative reaction, I would take immediate action. If I could, I'd stop what I was doing, unsubscribe, and delete the whole lot. If I couldn't stop, I'd jot down the name of the sender and go through that process later, when I did my nightly inbox purge.

For me, keeping up with virtual clutter is even harder than keeping up with actual clutter. When it comes to tangible possessions, I'm picky about what comes into my home in the first place (and I derive satisfaction when I send it out again when it ceases to be useful), but email is sneakier, arriving whether or not I'm at my computer and even when I'm asleep. Not only that but, when it comes to information, I'm all *I love stuff* all the time. I have a lifetime supply of books I want to read, and my current situation with emails is just as bad — worse, actually. Because emails don't take up physical space, I don't truly see them and so they accumulate in a way I'd never allow with physical clutter.

But I'm putting STYLE to work on my inbox:

Start with successes: No matter how small. (This plan is one of them).

Take small steps: I can't clear out my inbox overnight, but I can chip away at it.

Yes, it has a home: Use my filing system to find homes for the keepers.

Let it go: The action to take for unwanted emails/any that don't make me smile.

Easy upkeep: Reducing what comes in by unsub-scribing makes this a real thing.

Wish me luck.

True Confession #32: I am energized by progress.

LAST NIGHT, I picked up a book on life design* that I'd started quite a while ago. I'd left off in a section that talked about paying attention to the things that energize us or create flow for us — that wonderful feeling of being so absorbed in what we're doing that we lose all track of time. I'd tried to follow the instructions and keep a journal for a couple of days to help myself identify those things but, in the end, it went by the wayside.

At 50-something, I have a pretty good idea of what energizes me and what drains me, and organizing is (no surprise) one of the things that energizes me. But I'd never really taken the next step the authors recommend — zooming in to figure out what it is about organizing that I find so fulfilling.

So last night, I took that step. After putting the book down, I lay in bed, seeking my answer — one that arrived almost immediately and, conveniently enough, gave me the topic for this blog.

I am energized by progress.

This explains so much! Why I feel grumpy when I'm interrupted, why small steps work for me, why rediscovered (or newly created) clear space is so satisfying. Interruptions stop me (and my progress) short, leaving me frustrated (and therefore grumpy). Small steps lead to progress, even if it's just a start. And clear space? That's the ultimate proof of progress!

This "revelation" also explains why I love to write (fill up the blank screen with words!) and hate to revise (didn't I do this already??) Progress feels like smooth sailing. Anything else feels like a dirt road full of potholes.

I thought I was pretty good at creating a life that I find satisfying, something I've had a lot of practice doing since I hit reset on my career eight years ago. But this small piece of information gave me an opportunity to reframe my perspective, something the authors spend a lot of time on. For example, about ten seconds ago, I felt myself cringe when I heard the back door squeak open because that's often a sure sign that an interruption (a threat to progress) is on its way. Sure enough, footsteps followed...but they stopped short of the room where I am working.

Progress saved.

I often say that organizing is a process. But that process is built on progress — the small victories we find along the way. For this reason, it's essential to celebrate our progress, no matter how small, because that momentum is often what sustains us through the process.

How about you? Is there a part of organizing that energizes you? Why?

*In case you're wondering, the book on life design is
Designing Your Life
by Bill Burnett and Dave Evans.

True Confession #33: I organize on vacation.

LAST NIGHT, after I finished eating dinner, I dug into some more food — the supplies we brought along on vacation — but not because I was hungry. When we arrived last weekend, we plopped the tote full of snacks and supplies onto the kitchen counter, where it stayed. It seemed logical enough. Everything was contained in one spot rather than scattered haphazardly, but the set-up still bugged me. Add to that the pile-up in a corner of the dining room that made sense to my husband, but had me strategizing all through dinner and there was no way I was going to let the status quo go.

Half an hour later, I'd consolidated the stuff in the corner, repurposed a small corrugated tray from the bottled water as a coffee pod holder, and ditched the large box from the warehouse club that had previously been home to the coffee pods. I'd separated the food that had been opened from the food that had not, the breakfast food from the snack food, the gluten-free food from the rest and stored all the breads together. The tote became home to unopened containers and got stored off the counter, which then looked much, much better.

What I really needed was a container or two to maximize the space and make the categories clearer but, since our stay here is temporary, I drew the line at going out and purchasing containers.

Just barely.

I'm sure it seems silly that I concern myself with these things even on vacation, but I find it hard to relax when things look cluttered, especially when only a small fraction of our belongings is here in the first place. The condo where we stay has an open floor plan so when one area is cluttered,

it's really obvious. This trip, I even packed my reading material, writing stuff and miscellaneous entertainment in a bin
so that it was easy not only to find exactly what I wanted
when I wanted it, but to put it away when I was finished.

Right now, I've got my eye on three bags that, if they
were moved to a slightly different location, would be so
much less of an eyesore.

I think we all know where I'm going when I finish this
post.

True Confession #34: My house is a blend of order and chaos.

OKAY, maybe *chaos* is too strong a word, but, as I've said before, I'm a work in progress. That means that there are places in my house that are exactly as I want them to be and then there's....

The rest of the house.

While a couple of rooms are consistently under control, order and chaos often co-exist in other rooms. Since we have a small house, this means there may be a lovely, clear organized surface two feet away from an organizing challenge in the works.

My office is a prime example. I have conquered my desk, long an organizing challenge, and now it's usually cleared off unless I'm working there. On the other hand, the counter across the room (and "across the room" is a generous description) is a perpetual clutter magnet and the space in my house that comes closest to actual chaos. I make progress on a weekend, only to find that, by the end of the week, I've dumped new items there. It's a process, and not one I am winning.

While I'm a big fan of seizing small chunks of time to make progress, there are some areas that need either a continual succession of small chunks of time or a dedicated time block of an hour, an afternoon, or even a weekend.

I think my counter falls into that category.

Since I believe in taking small steps, and since I'm unlikely to have a totally free afternoon in which to tackle this organizing challenge, I'm going to set a small, approachable goal. Each day, I will spend at least 15 minutes de-cluttering my counter (even if that means three increments of five minutes each) until I whip it into the lovely, clear space I want it to be.

Long-time readers who are feeling a sense of déjà vu are not wrong. Seven years ago, I launched Operation: Clear the Counter and I made progress. But, in the past seven years, I've re-vamped, re-organized, and de-cluttered a lot of other spaces in my house and within the piles on my counter are items rendered homeless by those projects. Oh, and I retired, bringing all new piles home with me.

As someone who writes about organization and has mastered it in many areas, I don't like admitting to harboring chaos. This counter project is a big one — one that has the potential to be just the tip of the organizing iceberg — so I'm hoping my small steps will not only yield big successes but also help keep the frustration of tackling an enormous challenge at bay. And I'm hoping that going public will be yet another nudge to creating that Jerry Seinfeld calendar that truly does provide motivation.

Time to put some STYLE into action, fifteen minutes at a time.

True Confession #35: I'm an organizational multitasker.

WHEN IT COMES TO ORGANIZING, there are several varieties. There's the picking up and putting away of all the varied items that seem to walk out of closets and cabinets and plunk themselves on floors and surfaces *every single day*. There's the quick pick-up we do when company is coming in half an hour or less. There's the how-did-this-pile-get-so-big pick-up we do when things have accumulated on a countertop, desktop or table. And then there's the organizational overhaul, often kicked off by one of these smaller scale endeavors.

For me, summer is the time for organizational overhauls.

This summer, because I'm not teaching a class, I've rediscovered how much more leisurely my schedule can be. Suddenly, time, energy, and inclination to tackle problem areas have aligned, and I'm motivated to sort through accumulated items (mostly papers) and re-vamp the systems that have become overloaded due to a surplus of stuff. And, since I'm home more and need to devote less time to planning for classes, I'm noticing the less-than-stellar ways in which I deal with the things that don't have a home or a dedicated system.

In short? A pile of papers is not an organizational plan and a counter is not a storage container.

This summer, I targeted one trouble spot in particular: the counter in my office. In fact, in my last confession, I publicly promised to spend at least 15 minutes a day on it until it was free of piles and held only the things that were supposed to live there. When I got home from vacation, I even pulled out a calendar that had the whole year on one page so I could cross off each day, only to discover that it was a 2019 calendar and therefore easily disposed of. Writing this post reminded me of that, however, and I now have pressed a current calendar into service, crossing off Saturday, Sunday, Monday and yesterday and creating the beginning of my Jerry Seinfeld calendar.

As expected, the piles on the counter consist mostly of homeless items. This means I need to find places to put them. On Saturday night, after I spent my designated fifteen minutes on the counter (task #1), I sorted through two file bins that do not live on the counter (task #2), condensing them into one and freeing up the other. On Sunday night, I relocated some items displaced by the file bins sort (task #3), sorted through three containers holding contact information, tossed the old and put the ones that were still relevant into a business card file (which now needs a home). I used a picture frame on the counter to display post cards (also on the counter), which necessitated rearranging things I had on the walls in order to find a place to hang the frame (task #4). While most of this was part of the main job of clearing the counter, some of it was not.

Meanwhile, all of this occurred on the heels of our return from vacation. As I put away the bag I keep pre-packed with toiletries, I decided it was time to clean out the bin in which the bag lives (task #5). This led to more tossing, but also to uncovering more items that should be stored somewhere else, which led to taking a hard look at the top of my dresser (task #6), which has also become cluttered and in need of an overhaul.

When did all of this happen?

Life gets busy and, when it does, we revert to the habits at the root of our styles. If I ever doubted that I'm an *I need to see it/drop and run* kind of girl, one look at the top of my dresser or office counter is enough to send those doubts packing. And, when I see multiple areas in need of assistance, it's rarely a straight line from cluttered to clear.

Because I love to organize, I see all of this as an opportunity — a problem to be solved. And, since I have the time to tackle everything, I'm not overwhelmed but rather excited by the possibility of how things can look now that I've stopped looking past what needs to be done and am ready to dig in and do it.

My tendency to take on multiple projects simultaneously and redecorate as I reorganize definitely means it will all look worse before it looks better but, as someone with an *I need to see it* personal style, I recognize that all of those steps are a part of the process. And, as long as I stick to my promise to spend at least fifteen minutes a day chipping away at that counter, it's not really so terrible if I work on a few other things, too, just to keep things interesting. To avoid the drawbacks that accompany multitasking, I just need to make sure I focus on one area at a time, chunking my time instead of trying to do it all at once.

It's my process.

True Confession #36: I need time to let things evolve.

IN EDUCATION, we call this "think time" — the space we leave between a question we've posed and the answers our students provide. When it comes to organizing, it's the space between the start of a project and its completion, especially when we're taking small steps and working on something a little at a time.

That's exactly the approach I've been taking with the counter in my office. As promised here and to myself, I'm working on it for 15 minutes every day until I get it de-cluttered and looking nice. I've chipped away at it since we got home from the beach, missing only one day (but spending way more than 15 minutes on it on other days) and I'm discovering that the closer I get to finishing the project, the more think time I need.

Last night, for example, I don't think I got rid of anything. I'm down to one small pile of miscellaneous items, none of which is likely to be tossed and all of which need a home. Instead of tackling those decisions, I spent my 15+ minutes cleaning the counter and rearranging the decorative items that are vying for a place of honor on the finished space. Some might call this procrastination, and they wouldn't be entirely wrong.

But it's more than that. When I set the timer last night, the first thing that caught my eye was a mini display I'd created. It was too tall and, even though it was organized, it made the space look cluttered. So, I took it apart and played with the arrangement, moving this item and relocating that one and, in the end, the counter looked better than it had when I started, which is my only goal in my daily plan of attack.

If we want to organize in a sustainable way, we need to take our time, considering what belongs, what doesn't, what deserves a home, (even if it's somewhere else in the room or in the house), as well as what that home should look like. One reason I like taking small steps is that I'm more likely to remember what I put where and to create a space that's not only organized, but also pleasing to the eye. Because the line between the right amount of stuff and too much stuff can be very thin, this process takes time.

I'm happy with the gradual uncovering of clear space this project has yielded, and I enjoy hearing my family comment on it as well. But, once I've removed all the papers and clutter, I want the counter to look nice not just because it's clear, but because it's a reflection of the inhabitant of the space as well.

And that takes not only organizing time, but think time as well.

True Confession #37: If it's not broken, it's easy to ignore.

PILES. Closets so overstuffed the doors won't close. That mysterious smell coming from the back of the Mom-mobile. These things can't help but attract our attention. In fact, they practically scream for it, moving them to the top of our organizing to-do lists.

But what about the quieter spots? The cram-and-jam drawer that contains a little bit of everything, making it difficult to find anything? The stack of items to deal with later that got neatly tucked into a basket or bag, then a closet, leaving it out of sight and therefore out of mind? The surface that seems to be magnetized, based on the number of homeless items that have taken up residence there on a semi-permanent basis?

If the squeaky wheel gets the grease (no more clichés, I promise), these spots are doomed to a life of inattention — or at least a very long respite.

Whipping the counter in my office into shape made me more aware of these surfaces and spaces. The semi-empty file sorter on top of my desk. The top of the dresser in our bedroom. The top of the shoe organizer in my closet that began as a sort of vanity tabletop, but ended up a catchall for small, homeless items that kinda sorta belonged there.

What's going on here?

None of these spaces ever had a pile dumped into or on top of them. Each one started as a clear space that slowly morphed into a holding zone for a variety of homeless items, usually one at a time, that were supposed to be there temporarily until slowly, but surely, each of these clear spaces stopped being clear and became a catch-all space. It happened gradually and stayed just under the radar until it reached the tipping point.

But that third spot — the one inside my closet — was the sneakiest one. As with decorative baskets and junk drawers and yes, the file sorter on my desk, the stuff was hidden away. Those spots didn't call out to me like the counter in my office or the top of my dresser. They just quietly collected stuff.

And dust.

While part of the problem here is my *I need to see it* personal style, there's also something deeper at work.

None of those spots was assigned a definite purpose. That set them up perfectly to catch the overflow until they, too, overflowed. Until they reached that tipping point (or my consciousness was raised, thanks to my counter), they were easy enough to ignore.

When we see things that are out of place, we are motivated to put them back — maybe not immediately, but eventually. But, when something is out of place for too long, it begins to claim that space as its own and we no longer notice that it's not where it belongs. And, if a place isn't assigned a purpose — this shelf holds books, this cabinet holds pots and pans, this basket holds toiletries — it becomes a magnet for things that aren't assigned a home.

My office counter is much, much better, with almost every last homeless item removed from it and given a home. Right now, I'm taking think time as I try to decide how many of the decorations that are there get to stay. I might also solicit opinions from my husband and daughter about what looks cluttered to them and use their input to rearrange some things into the final configuration of the space but first, I'll do what I did to the top of the shoe organizer in the closet.

I will clear off the counter completely, clean it, and put

things back one at a time, paying attention to what is enough and what is too much, trying to find the tipping point. Right now, though I am loving the expanse of open space, I can tell there is more work to be done.

When it comes to organization, some of our projects call out to us. The ones to be wary of, however, are the ones that serve as quiet collectors.

True Confession #38: Sometimes, I need a "look around" day.

I HAVE a quote posted in my office that says, "Happiness is found along the way, not at the end of the road." With apologies to the author which, according to the Internet, is Robert Updegraff, I would argue that sometimes, organization is found along the way, not at the end of the road.

Lately, I've been very list-driven. This *sounds* like a good thing but, if you're a recovering perfectionist like me, it's really only a good thing if you actually get to the bottom of the list (which I rarely do). In an ongoing effort to divorce myself from workaholism and recapture my weekends, I've been trying to keep my Saturday and Sunday lists more flexible so that I'm more flexible, too.

Last Saturday, I ditched the list and took what I started calling a "look around" day (and yes, I hear Renée Elise Goldsberry's voice singing that, which makes it even more fun).

Look around. What do you see? What needs to be done? What do you want to tackle first? Those were the questions that formed my mental list on Saturday and, you know what?

I got a lot done.

When I looked around, all the little hidden hot spots -- the "quiet collectors" that don't make it to the list — came into focus. Sure, the obvious stuff jumped out, too, but most of those spots make it onto the lists I create all week long. If free-flow weekends are the balance to structured week days, then a "look around" Saturday was a perfect fit.

In many cases, the things that jumped out were the little things that annoyed me every time I walked by them — a succession of small spots of clutter that I disregarded (kind of) because I was trying to stay focused on "the list." Most required less than fifteen minutes of my attention which, on a focus-on-the-list day was enough to pull me off-track. But, on a "look around" day, they *were* the list, the track — the whole shebang.

In organizing, as in life, we sometimes need to step back and look at the whole picture before we zoom in and pour all of our time and energy into one small piece of the puzzle. "Look around" days help us prioritize in a different way, giving us permission to do what we want to do, to focus our attention on the thing that nags at us, even if no one else notices it.

I've said (repeatedly) that organizing is a process, but it's also a matter of balance — balancing the big, must-do tasks with smaller tasks that can actually be more personally satisfying. Tackling all the little things that screamed for my attention every time I walked by them actually set me up for a week where it was easier to focus because there were fewer distractions. And now, when things call out to me during the week, I know I can choose to tackle them immediately, put them on the list, or save them for "Look Around Saturday," which I might just make a regular occurrence.

In fact, I know the perfect soundtrack to accompany it.

True confession #39: I respect professional organizers, but I don't always agree with them.

LAST WEEK, I read a great article about decluttering, aimed at older aduts, an audience who's in a downsizing time of life. While I didn't agree with every recommendation, I thought it was a great piece because with ten potential starting points, most of us can easily find a place to dig in.

As a voracious reader on the topic of organization, I've seen many of these tips before. Because I know organizing by STYLE works for me, I did what I always do when I read one of these articles. I put all ten of them through my *I need to see it/drop and run* filter.

1. Books you won't read again. *Agree.* Sometimes I'm successful in putting a book directly into the giveaway pile when I finish it. Other times, they languish on my shelves, taking up space until I either run out of space or review my choices in my annual Christmas purge. Either way, they go into a bag I can take to my local library, which accepts book donations — at least when we're not in the midst of a pandemic.

2. Clothes you or your family has outgrown. *Agree.* Consign, sell or donate the best, toss the rest.

3. Movies and music on CD, DVD, or anything else. *Agree to disagree.* The article recommends going digital (good plan) and/or replacing the cases with less bulky storage. Whether or not the latter suggestion makes sense depends on the size of your collection, your storage space and, of course, your styles. While I can't argue that there are more streamlined solutions than plastic cases, I will argue that, right now at least, my storage for these items works for me and my styles and protects my investment without intruding into my home.

4. Old, expired canned good. *Completely agree.* In addition, this is a great starting point because the decision is black and white. Something either is expired or it isn't.

5. Obsolete gadgets, electronics, and appliances. *Agree.* For these items, the question is where to take them. Most of ours end up at Best Buy, which has recycled pretty much everything we've ever wanted to get rid of. If you'd like to do more than recycle your old cell phone, programs like Cell Phones for Soldiers and Recycling for Charities recycle the technology for a cause. In addition, some carriers will buy back your cell phone or use its value toward the purchase of a new one. If you're disposing of electronics, always check local regulations to see what can and cannot safely go into the trash.

6. Papers, please. *Agree and disagree.* As someone with an ***I need to see it*** personal style, I struggle to find the sweet spot between hard copies and electronic copies. When it comes to some things, I will always be a paper girl.

7. Faded photos. *Agree.* While I'm not advocating a purge of photo albums (nor was the article), I know that tossing just duplicate, out-of-focus, and "who is this person?" photos would significantly reduce my photo pile. Here again, the battle between printed photos and digital copies at my house is ongoing.

8. Knickknacks and doodads-a-plenty. *Agree...kind of.* This one hits home for me. While part of me longs for clear spaces, the rest of me is sentimental enough to hang on to all kinds of things others would part with in a millisecond. As with anything else, duplicates (how many key rings or magnets do I really need?) and anything that takes up space without also meaning something to its owner can be the first to go.

9. Large, oversized furniture. *Agree to disagree.* For me, the comfort factor outweighs the space factor. I'd toss our dining room chairs in the trash before I'd get rid of the chairs from my parents' house — the ones that are living in the basement because there's no room in our living space for them. Definitely not logical on some levels, but when I finally sit down to relax, I want to be comfortable.

10. Anything else that's not nailed down. *Agree.* The writer went on to explain this as a catch-all category, rather than a literal suggestion, citing the "when's the last time this was used?" argument — a valid question, even if it's not the only criteria for hanging on to something or getting rid of it.

How did these tips fare in your style filter? While they're a great starting point for anyone looking to tackle the L of STYLE ("Let it go!"), the suggestions in articles like these they won't fit every style. They can, however, provide us with the nudge we need to start somewhere.

And that's often the hardest part of the process.

The post for Confession #39 was inspired by an article in Next Avenue called "Declutter Your Home: 10 Things You Can Throw Out Now."

True confession #40: I am a serial organizer.

HAVE you ever seen the *Golden Girls* episode where the girls ask Sophia what she did that day and she says, "What did I do today? I did what I do every day. I bought a nectarine." The full episode, which includes Sophia's point-of-view alongside the girls' perspective, reveals that Sophia did much, much more.

Often, we look at our days and underestimate our accomplishments. One of the reasons I love taking small steps when I tackle an organizing project is that most of my projects turn out to be bigger than I expected them to be.

Take my most recent project: organizing magazines and creating a clipping file. This actually emerged from my desire to empty a basket full of reading materials that I hadn't touched in ages.

The first step was easy enough — sort the basket — and I knew that would take more than one session. The basket was deep and full of magazines, each of which takes up very little space, which means that basket housed a *lot* of magazines. Once upon a time, that was a selling point. Now, I recognize that basket as an *I need to see it* stumbling block.

But I digress.

Unsatisfied merely sorting the magazines and clippings, I decided to gather up the homeless magazines that were sitting on surfaces and add them to the pile.

See what I did there? I complicated matters from the very first step. My aim was to be thorough but, by doing this, I lengthened the process and, by extension, the amount of time it would take to complete it.

By the time I was (mostly) finished this (multi-day) project, I'd gone from the basket to the bookshelf in the living room to the bookshelf in the mudroom to the magazine baskets in various locations to the bins of reading material, also in the living room. Each was emptied, sorted, and its contents put into a (newly) designated location.

In the process of doing this project, I identified my target areas (the containers that needed to be sorted), evaluated my containers, and looked on Pinterest for magazine storage ideas. (I rejected most of what I found — they looked nice, but my goal was to reduce the stacks not just make what I had look better). I considered all the possible reading material storage areas in my house (thus the trek from basket to bookshelf to bin and back) and ended up cleaning those out, too. I sorted magazines by title and designated logical homes for everything, based on how much space they took up and how long I expected to keep them.

Every single one of these things could be a single small step — a single session, or part of longer one.

For me, they were a combination. I have a lot of reading material. The good news is that nearly everything (except for a few things left to be sorted this weekend) now has a logical home that fits my organizing and reading habits. I know where everything is and I know where everything goes.

What did I do for the last two weekends? I cleared out a basket.

If you'll forgive another '80s reference, The Fixx was right. One thing *does* lead to another.

True confession #41: I have organizing rules.

LAST WEEK, I shared my adventures in magazine and book sorting, all of which emerged from my desire to clear out a basket, get rid of some old magazines and create a clipping file. I've made a little more progress, but I'm beginning to think my magazines reproduce when I'm not around.

In the end, sorting the basket (where this project began) was the tip of the iceberg. I knew I didn't want to put things back into the basket when I was finished because that would just start the cycle all over again. As someone with an *I need to see it* personal style, I knew that once the reading material landed in the bottom of the basket, I was unlikely to pay any further attention to it, especially as I continued to pile new material on top of the old stuff, obscuring it from view. Things would *look* organized, but they wouldn't actually *be* organized; instead, they'd just be neatly piled and hidden from view, which made them more likely to be ignored than enjoyed.

In order to get to **E**asy Upkeep, I needed a home for the clippings that made them easy to access and a home for the magazines that kept them visible *and* easily accessible. Why didn't the clippings need to be visible? Because they're reference materials that can be archived.

These may sound like random rules but they are at the heart of organizing by STYLE. As someone with an *I need to see it* personal style, I know that I need to keep active items (magazines to be read) where I can see them. Archived items (clippings and other reference materials) can be kept out of sight, but need a consistent, organized home so they can go from unseen to seen quickly and easily.

Huh?

Despite my personal style, I can't leave everything

where I can see it — that would be chaos. Consequently, I need to be selective about what truly stays visible, what gets placed into eye-catching homes and what can be put away (but kept color-coded, labeled, or similarly organized) until I really need it.

Truly visible? Anything used frequently or that needs to be attended to immediately. "Frequently" is tough to define, but includes anything used daily. Items used less often are a judgment call, but most likely fall into the second category....

Stored in an I need to see it fashion. Things that need to be referenced, but aren't used often can actually go out of sight, but need to take my styles into account so they can be easily put away and easily accessed.

My clippings ended up in a dedicated bin with lid, filed in labeled, color-coded file folders. Why a bin and not a file cabinet? Because it's easier to lift the lid and drop the clippings in, which suits my *drop and run* organizational style.

I have to say that very few of my organizing projects get this complicated but, when it comes to reading material, I have a lot of it. And, as someone whose professional home base *is* her home, I set out to create a system that made it easy to access leisure reading, work reading and the myriad items that live on the line between the two categories.

One last note. Every bin/container/shelf/piece of furniture that houses my reading material has a little room for me to add new items, but not so much space that things can get out of control. This means that, in order for the system to keep working, I need to stay on top of the contents and get rid of outdated material and things that no longer interest me.

This domino project is almost finished and I'm happy to say that I haven't resorted to tossing random and/or homeless items back into the basket. Though it was a challenge to find consistent, logical homes for everything from clippings to books I want to read, I no longer have the feeling that magazines I stashed somewhere "safe" are lying in wait. They've all been brought out into the light and dealt with — some made the cut, some did not — and it felt good to let a lot of them go. Finally, because I have a system that makes sense to me, I know just where to find the ones I want when I need them.

It was a long, circuitous path, but I think I've arrived at **E**asy upkeep, and I like the view.

True Confession #42: I'm currently in a "struggling to juggle"phase.

I HEARD a rumor that there are people who are bored from too much time at home. Others have run out of things to watch on television. I can promise you that none of those people are teachers at any grade level or parents of school-aged (or younger) children, unless, perhaps, they have tutors and domestic help. Some days, we feel as though we're in a bad episode of *Candid Camera* but bored? Not even close.

I cannot remember the last weekday when a nap was not essential if I intended to be even remotely human for the rest of the day. In fact, as I type this, I'm trying to decide if I want to stop typing *right now* or take a nap after I post this. Either way, sleep is in the equation, sooner rather than later.

I've always lived right on the edge of the line between *I need to see it* and *I love to be busy*, but I didn't bargain on the learning curve that came with the busyness this fall. And whether it's a learning curve that requires ropes and pulleys, a schedule that leaves you hanging on for dear life, or simply a little too much reality, these are the times when our best-laid organizational schemes begin to show wear and tear. And, as for our organizational weak spots? They start falling apart at the seams.

My beautifully clear counter? A repository for my class planning materials. My almost-always clear mail counter? About a week behind. My to-do lists? Scraps of paper that I'm afraid to transfer to one list because I fear it will be longer than I am tall.

My mantra for these times has become "one thing at a time," or, some days, "all in good time." (And some days, "I can't even look at that right now.") Not original, I know, but the first two bear repeating, at least until I get into a routine befitting the latest rendition of the new normal.

How do we know where to start when it seems that everything is calling to us? That will depend on our styles. As someone with an *I need to see it* personal style, I knew I needed to reduce the visual clutter because visual overload increases my stress level and decreases my productivity. A *cram and jam*mer might need to take action when a container is overflowing, while someone with an *I love to be busy* personal style may take a break because the slots on her calendar are overflowing. The *I love stuff* person may be unable to find her favorite treasure (or may need a home for a new one), while the *drop and run* organizer may no longer be able to follow his trail and the *I know I put it somewhere* organizer reaches the organizing breaking point after putting one thing too many in a safe place.

Whether you start with what's most frustrating, most obvious, or most time sensitive, keep in mind that this, too, shall pass. And, until it does, being patient with yourself and doing what you can is the best way to take small steps that can lead you in the right direction.

For me, that direction was the restoration of the counter in my office. Last weekend, I came up with a plan that let me see things and keep them organized, but required a significantly smaller footprint. In addition, I transferred some of the materials I'm finished with into what will be archival storage. The rest will have to wait until this week-end, unless I manage to eke out a few five-to-fifteen-minute slots between now and then. Either way, I'm excited to be on the path to clear space again.

Now, if you'll excuse me, I am quite certain that I've earned my nap.

True Confession #43: I am a last minute packer.

IT MAKES no difference how much lead time I have. It makes little difference how busy I am (although that is a factor). When it comes to packing, I am always putting things together the night before we leave.

And the day of departure.

International trips notwithstanding, my clothes don't go in my suitcase until the last possible minute. I start mental preparations ahead of time, and do lots of laundry basket packing (clean clothes come upstairs and the ones I'm thinking of taking along go into a laundry basket in my bedroom) but rarely do things make it into a suitcase sooner than the night before.

Procrastination is definitely a factor, as is experience, but the most important factor that lets me get away with this is the fact that I have a process.

- **Pre-Pack**. With the exception of make-up and medicine, all of my toiletries are always packed. And long before I put anything in a suitcase, I'm making lists and tossing odds and ends into bags (and that laundry basket) so I don't forget to pack them.
- **Pack as I go/stash it when I think of it.** I always pack make-up and medicine the day I leave, immediately after I use it. That way, I'm less likely to forget something I need. At times (like now) when I'm busy, I pull contenders for the suitcase out as I get dressed. One sweater to put on, another to pack.

- **Develop a routine.** For me, it's laying everything out on a flat surface where I can see it, which makes it much easier for me to figure out what I have and what's missing. (I also make lists). To my husband, my plan looks like chaos, but it works for me, so I stand by it. Likewise, your plan doesn't have to make sense to anybody else; it just has to work for you.

I certainly don't recommend waiting until the last minute to get everything together. But, if you find yourself in that situation, as I so often do, getting it together successfully is possible.

Especially if you have a process.

True confession #44: I am terrible at estimating how long things take.

ONE OF THE pieces of advice often offered by those who do time management well is to estimate how long a task will take, then add at least fifteen minutes. Others suggest building buffer time between tasks to aid in staying on schedule.

I don't know if I'm optimistic or dense, but no matter how I try, I cannot manage to do this successfully on a regular basis. I have my regular routines down so that I am rarely late for obligations (like work) but, when it comes to things like getting ready to leave for (or from) a trip, I always cut things too close. I considered the possibility that this happens only when it's something I don't want to do (like pack or leave for home after a weekend away), but my internal monologue is always the same.

It won't take that long.

Ha. Famous last words. It *always* takes longer than I think it will.

I'd like to say I'll do better — or, better yet, actually *do* better — and I probably will on a limited basis. The real problem, I suspect, lies in transitions. When I'm happily ensconced in an activity, it's easy to convince myself that the thing I have to next won't take as long as I think it will because I don't want to stop doing the thing I'm already doing.

Just me?

In the end, I'm on time for most things that matter and I'm good at cramming a lot of tasks into a day when I put my mind to it but, if the option for flex-time exists, I'll take it every time.

How about you? Are you good at sticking to a schedule, or are you hoping someone will create a planner with dotted lines to accommodate your style of one activity merging into the next?

True Confession #45: I'm not good at counting my successes.

I'M DEFINITELY A LIST MAKER, and I love checking things off those lists but, instead of focusing on what I checked off, I instead find myself frustrated by the items that remain.

Part of the problem is that I tend to overpack my lists. In the interest of writing everything down, I lose sight of the fact that the amount of space in the Monday box on my week-at-a-glance planner isn't necessarily a good indication of whether or not there are actually enough hours in Monday to get it all done.

In the past few months, I've checked a few things off my long-term list, including finally getting rid of the file cabinet in my office and replacing it with storage that's a better fit for my *I need to see it* personal style and actually keeping the desk and counter in my office mostly clear on a regular basis. I've also come up with a simple, style-friendly way to keep track of my class planning materials without them taking over either of those clear spaces. All of these things led to a tidier, more efficient office space but, some days, when I look around, all I see is what remains to be done — here and everywhere else in the house.

Isn't my first rule of STYLE **S**tart with successes?

Indeed it is. And the irony of this does not escape me. I stand by that starting point, too, but that doesn't mean it's always easy. It takes special effort to notice our successes amid a never-ending backdrop of things to be done or clear spaces to be reclaimed from the detritus of day-to-day life.

It's really important to notice these things, though, because our successes are what keep us going, reminding us of what we're capable of, perhaps most of all during those times when we feel less-than-capable.

So, I'm going to close with a little lesson in reframing. (Some might call it rationalization. I prefer to classify it as reclaiming success from perceived failure).

It's Thursday. This is (clearly) a Wednesday post, one that was unfinished as Wednesday turned into Thursday. I have several choices. I can abandon it and delete it, negating the work that went into it and leaving an empty space on this blog where a Wednesday post might have been. I can skip this week, and save it for next week, posting it on the right day of the week.

Or, I can post it today.

All of these options are viable, and it's up to me to decide which choice to make. The empty space will disappear quickly, as soon as I post something new, and future readers will perhaps not even notice that this week, there was no Wednesday post.

But that option isn't the one that makes me feel successful. A post that's late seems to me to be better than no post at all and so up this one will go. Today.

Sometimes, success is in the eye of the beholder.

Even if she needs a magnifying glass to find it.

True Confession #46: I struggle with the transition from one month to the next.

I CAN HARDLY BELIEVE the end of the month is almost upon us! At school, in particular, this gets my attention because this year, fall semester ends on the Tuesday before Thanksgiving. It's been a challenging semester on many levels and compacting it has been one of those challenges.

As someone with an *I need to see it* personal style, it's the flip of the calendar page that gets me. Yes, I'm aware of how ridiculous that sounds coming from a full-grown woman but, somehow, a week that is split between one month and the next contributes to my losing track of time in a way I can't really explain.

Luckily, this month will not provide the same challenge since the last week of the month had the courtesy to fill an entire row of blocks on my calendar page. But, since other months are less cooperative, I've come up with a few tips that help to keep the shock of "you mean that's *next* week?" at bay. They're not foolproof, but their consistent use has kept me from missing many important events and appointments.

Look ahead. Preparing for a transition makes it easier, and the simplest way for me to do this is to make it a habit to flip from one month to the next far enough ahead of time to wrap my brain around the wraparound of this month into next. Ten days to two weeks ahead of time is usually sufficient.

Create a sign post. Always meaning to look ahead but still getting caught by surprise? Jot important first-week-of-the-next-month tasks or appointments on a small, square sticky note and attach it to a calendar square in the last week of the month.

Do a weekly check-in. My family just loves this (yes, that's sarcasm), but it helps us to make sure that we align our calendars and don't miss appointments (plus my husband is better at the whole next-week-is-a-new-month thing than I am). When my daughter was growing up, we had our "calendar meeting" at dinner on Friday, but you can pencil in any time that works for your family. Once this becomes a habit, it's something that can be accomplished in less than ten minutes.

Investing a little time in your calendar can make things run more smoothly every day of the month, even when the next one sneaks up on you.

True confession #47: Organizing feeds my problem-solving side.

I DON'T KNOW why it took me so long to figure this out but, there you have it. I love how organizing helps me begin with chaos, brainstorm a solution, put it into action, and end up with order.

From this perspective, organizing by STYLE was a game changer because it gave me a lens through which to view both the clutter and the eventual solution. Knowing something about how things need to look when I'm finished (I need to see them and I need to be able to put them away quickly, often on my way to the "next thing") makes it easier to get from order to chaos. In addition, I love the challenge of finding the "just right" container — one that fits the space, serves the purpose, and looks good in the process. Best of all, I love the clear space that results when the clutter gets sorted, the excess gets purged, and the treasures get put away.

It's a wonderful feeling of accomplishment.

But, the true test of any solution is whether or not it's sustainable long-term. Some spots require a bit of trial and error while others are easily whipped into shape. When that happens, I'm one step closer to my unattainable goal: a perfectly organized life.

A girl can dream.

True Confession #48: Sometimes, it's hard to accept our styles.

ALTHOUGH THE HEART of organizing by style is embracing our default styles and building from there, let's face it: sometimes, it's hard to let go of what we think we *should* be doing. When we come up against an organizing challenge and someone suggests a tried-and-true tool like a binder or a file cabinet, we might be comfortable saying they don't work for us, but still a bit sensitive to the eye-roll or argument that may follow.

I mean, those tools work for everyone, right?

Only they don't. And finding what does can be a challenge. It can require reconfigurations that we love but others don't understand. (Just ask my husband what he thinks of my open-top files in the family room). It can reinforce the idea that, for us, organizing hasn't always been second-nature.

Only it can be.

I've been organizing by style for thirteen years and I don't miss filing cabinets at all. In fact, I've even been known to invite the occasional pretty, visually appealing binder back into my office, provided it follows my rules. And, while I still revert to piling when things get busy or I'm in the middle of an organizing project, I recognize that it's a temporary stopgap measure, not an organizational system. Most of all, I protect clear space now with a ferocity I didn't know I had when it came to organization, and I'm immune to the eyeballs of my audience when I do so.

Never come between a Jersey girl and her clear space.

I know I've said it hundreds of times before, but organizing is a process. But, the process of accepting ourselves as we are — whether it comes to organizing or anything else — isn't always easy or fast.

So, let me ask you this: is organizing by style working for you? If it is, keep doing what you're doing because it only gets easier with practice.

And, while you're at it, tell that inner voice that's making it hard for you to accept your styles (Your parents? Your sixth grade teacher? That girl in your math class who always had everything together and got straight As?) that you've got this.

The more you tell them, and the better you get at this, the more you'll believe it, and the better you'll get at strengthening perhaps the most important organizing tool of all.

Self-confidence.

You've got this.

True confession #49: I organize for fun.

IF YOU READ this blog regularly, I'm sure this doesn't come as a surprise, especially since I recently wrote about how much I enjoy the problem-solving aspect of organizing.

During one of the last Sundays of the semester, as I struggled to figure out what remained to be done in each class and how I needed to organize the content, I found myself getting crabbier and crabbier. I knew I needed a break, but I didn't want to start something I'd get pulled into and not want to stop doing. So, I set a timer for fifteen minutes and dug into the box of files behind my desk (more on that later). Fifteen minutes, an overstuffed trash can (I was rather ruthless), a handful of recycling, and eleven empty file folders later, I actually did feel better.

Lighter.

Sorting and purging has that effect on me.

The box in question is just one of several hot spots that have cropped up in the past month as I struggled to balance end-of-semester tasks with the onset of holiday decorating and an influx of Santa-related packages. The box of files — the largest and most intrusive of the piles — is the last remnant of an office revamp that relegated my long-neglected file cabinet to the basement (where archival storage belongs). While it would have been easier to just put everything back in the drawers, I wasn't convinced I needed everything that was in the drawers, especially since I couldn't actually remember the last time I'd looked at anything inside the drawers. So, I'd tossed all the files into a box, planning to sort through it a few files at a time and create a filing system more in line with what I need now.

It was a good plan in theory, but you know what

happens to the best-laid plans. And what road good intentions pave.

So, the box, along with its smaller, less-contained counterparts, has been calling out to me for the past couple of weeks, each stack doing its part to distract me from the more time-sensitive tasks at hand. But now, with the bulk of those tasks checked off my list, the fun part has arrived.

I get to organize.

To make things even more fun, I have my pick of the projects. Last night, I got started on some of the papers in my office that needed to be sorted and filed (in addition to the box of files). I also need to find a way to organize the books and papers I'm accumulating as I plan to teach a newish (taught for the first and last time two years ago) course this spring.

I have a kitchen cabinet overhaul to do, thanks to a splurge on new dishes, along with new pots and pans to go with the (necessary) new stove. Most of the cookware has found a home, but I need to do a little more thinking about the right homes for a few sentimental items taken from my mom's cupboards that have been displaced by the changes.

Oh, and there's Christmas decorating, along with finding temporary homes for everything displaced (are you sensing a theme here?) by the Christmas stuff. And Christmas presents I dare not use an *I know I put it somewhere* approach with or I'll be giving them out on St. Patrick's Day.

While some would find all of this overwhelming, I (mostly) find it exciting. So many possibilities for purging things I no longer need and creating clear space!

Thanks to a combination of better habits and a largely paper-free semester, things look much better (kitchen changes notwithstanding) than they have at the end of previous semesters. One personal victory is my desk, which

I have consistently cleared off each night for a record number of months. This is a success that has not only sustained me, but motivated me to keep other clear spaces clear as well.

When things get busy, it's easy to fall into the piling habit, especially for those of us who have *I need to see it* personal styles and/or *drop and run* organizational styles. But, with a success or two to remind us of what we can do when the dust settles, and the availability of time, whether blocks or snippets, organizing can be something we look forward to.

Lemme at those piles.

True Confession #50: For me, taking small steps has many benefits.

AT THE END of every semester, there are things to organize. Because I collected no physical papers this semester, there were fewer things to file but, because I have an *I need to see it* personal style, things were hardly paperless. Consequently, one of my first endeavors at the end of the semester is to tie up loose ends and put everything away, preferably in a place where it will be easy to access.

Inevitably, this leads to a reorganization of my (home) office as well. Because of the pandemic, my campus visits were direct and as brief as possible. Put on my mask, walk to class, teach, and leave. Other than a once-weekly visit to my mailbox, that was it. I visited my on-campus office only once all semester, to check for a book I needed. As a result, everything I needed for class, from textbooks to the last little note jotted on a scrap of paper, lived in my home office.

No matter how well-organized I am throughout the semester, things get hectic in the final crunch, leading to lots of those little notes to myself — things to remember, things to do differently (or again) next semester, new resources to check out. I plan my weeks on paper, too, as I *really* need to see it when I'm sketching out readings, discussions and assignments.

When I set up my system at the start of the semester (a single drop spot for everything I used on a regular basis, in keeping with my *drop and run* organizational style), it "lived" on the counter in my office. After a while, though, that started to bug me. I'd worked hard to clear off that counter and, the bin, while organizationally useful, had a rather large footprint. I moved it to the floor, which was also not a great solution, but it was accessible and I figured I'd deal with it at the end of the semester.

Which arrived two weeks ago. It was time.

So, for the past two weeks, I've been chipping away, one scrap of paper and project at a time, blurring the already fuzzy line between organizing and decorating, with the goal of creating a space I want to spend time in. Integrating the bin into my existing systems was the first step and, in a small office, it was more giant step than baby step. Plan A didn't work, but it resulted in a new configuration for the top of my desk. This led to the purchase of a long-sought-after clip-on lamp to resolve the lighting issue that had become even more apparent with the advent of Zoom sessions. The reconfiguration also led to me taking a file sorter that was more decorative than functional (and was therefore not earning its keep) and pressing it into service, so that it now does more than look pretty.

Next up was the small, round table imported from my parents' house. Its portability gives me the functionality of the L-shaped desk I crave, but that won't fit into my tiny office. This only works, however, when it's not littered with a collection of notes and reading material, so that was step two.

In the process of all this weeding, clearing and filing, it's become evident that I need a better system for my many writing projects and ideas as well. And, as I mentioned in my last confession, I also need a home for all the materials I'm gathering for a newish class I'm teaching next semester. These projects are next up. They'll not only help me feel less scattered, but they also have the added advantage of allowing me to procrastinate. The file box with the contents of my relocated file cabinet will be the last to go, unless I make good on developing the habit of clearing out three files after dinner at least three times a week.

At five feet nothing and with limited athletic prowess, I'm not much of a volleyball player. I do, however, remember the concept of rotating so that everyone on the team gets a chance to serve, and it comes to mind every time I do one of these office mini-makeovers. I almost always have everything I need, but, at the end of the process, many existing team members have taken on new roles.

Though it sometimes frustrates me that I never seem to be "finished," I'm beginning to accept that as a reflection of a life that continues to grow and change, and that's a very good thing. Taking this process step-by-step and doing it in multiple sessions not only gives me a chance to absorb the changes so I can remember where things are, it builds in a way to weed out the old to make room for the new. For every item that needs to claim its space, there's one (or more) to get rid of, and, next to clear spaces, that's the part of organization that I like best.

In the final weeks of the semester, I'd begun to dread walking into my office at home. Doing so only made me long for a day when I could grab a book to read for fun and go wherever I wanted in the house to enjoy doing just that. For the past week, I've loved walking into my office. Part of that clearly has to to with the fact that my fall semester tasks are complete, but much of it has to do with the fact that I've reclaimed the space as an organized oasis — or at least made significant progress in that direction.

Life brings its hectic times, but it also brings us opportunities to recover, even if the balance feels far from perfect. Within those routines — or the lack thereof — we find turning points that can spark our desire to purge, to clear, to grow and to organize.

What are your turning points?

Want more?

Check out my other posts at Organizing by STYLE (www. orgbystyle.blogspot.com). Or, for something a little more pulled together, you might enjoy my book Know Thyself: The Imperfectionist's Guide to Sorting Your Stuff.

Additional credits:
Cute ducks on the cover: Monika P. via Pixabay
Cover created with Canva